# Getting to Know
# the Bible

# Getting to Know the Bible

## An Introduction to Sacred Scripture for Catholics

**Rev. Melvin L. Farrell, S.S.**

**Revised by Joseph McHugh**

ASSISTING CHRISTIANS TO ACT

PUBLICATIONS

*Getting to Know the Bible*
*An Introduction to Sacred Scripture for Catholics*
by Rev. Melvin L. Farrell, S.S.
revised by Joseph McHugh

Edited by Kass Dotterweich
Cover design by Tom A. Wright
Typesetting by Desktop Edit Shop, Inc.

Published by:    ACTA Publications
                 Assisting Christians To Act
                 4848 N. Clark Street
                 Chicago, IL 60640
                 800-397-2282
                 actapublications@aol.com
                 www.actapublications.com

Library of Congress Catalog number: 2003104387

ISBN: 0-87946-247-7

Printed in the United States of America

Year: 10 09 08 07 06 05 04 03
Printing: 10 9 8 7 6 5 4 3 2 1

# Contents

## Part II
## The New Testament

# Introduction

Aclassic definition of the Bible is "the Word of God in the words of human beings." Thus the Scriptures are both divinely inspired and humanly composed—and both aspects are essential. This definition, however, raises two critical questions: How are the books of the Bible the Word of God? And how are the books of the Bible the words of human beings?

## The Word of God

How are the books of the Bible the Word of God? First and foremost, they tell how God makes himself and his intentions known by means of events or historical happenings. Examples include the Exodus, God's freeing of the Israelites from Egypt under Moses, and the Resurrection, God's raising of Jesus to life after his death.

Second, the books of the Bible are about how God's revelation is to be found in an ongoing way within the community of believers that comes into being as a result of his saving actions. This community not only keeps alive the memory of God's past actions on its behalf but also relies on the presence and action of God in its midst, day to day, in order to know and do his will. The Exodus gave rise to a religious people, the Hebrews (later called the Jews)—a people who believe they have been the direct beneficiaries of God's saving action. The Christian Church came into existence as a people who believe that God offers salvation to all through Jesus' death and resurrection. From the start, both religious communities believed God was with them in an abiding way, directing their life, worship and faith understanding—and this remains true today. God's initial revelation through saving events endures through time in the guidance he continues to provide the community of believers. The Bible is an integral part of the faith community whose origins it reflects and within which it came to light.

Thus God inspired authors to give written form to the message of salvation he was communicating to his people. Over the centuries, this Word of God has taken the form of written material, which we call the Bible.

## The Word of Human Beings

We now turn to an equally important question: How are the books of the Bible the words of human beings? From a human point of view, there was nothing miraculous about how the books of the Bible were written. God did not put the authors into a trance. He did not whisper in their ears nor did he give them any private or direct revelation. Rather, God fully honored the unique personhood of each writer. Each wrote as you or I would write, using ordinary processes of composition. Although they were limited to their own vocabulary, knowledge and creative ability, they were personally motivated to write and consciously chose the form and plan of their writings.

Just as it is important to pay attention to the human authorship of the Scriptures, it is also important to know something about the historical setting for each book. We have to ask questions such as when was it written, why was it written, for whom was it written. The material in the New Testament was produced roughly two to seven decades after the life, death and resurrection of Jesus. In the case of the Old Testament, the gap between the events and the written accounts of those events was often several centuries.

We also need to ask about *how* each book was written. Technically, this is a question of the literary form of each book. We are familiar with many literary forms in modern writing, and our understanding of a work's form enables us to properly understand its content. We know literary forms such as poetry, short story, romance, western and war novel. Even in newspapers we recognize several forms, including reporting, editorials, advertisements and comic strips. Each follows its own laws of composition, and each is a literary form in its own right.

Literary forms vary from culture to culture and from age to age. We cannot assume that the literary form of an ancient work has an exact counterpart among our modern ones. Sometimes we must acknowledge that the piece we are reading follows laws of composition that are strange to us. To understand the work correctly we must first acquaint ourselves with the literary form.

The various types of literary forms used in the Bible do not change the significance of any individual work. The books are always the Word of God. But having a grasp of the literary form employed by the human author helps us realize how God's Word comes to us and how it is to be interpreted. This can make a significant difference in our understanding.

## The Real Author

So thoroughly human was the work of each author whose writing is contained in the Bible that it is a wonder we call the results the Word of God at all. Yet we do. God so intimately involved himself in the total process of the Bible's composition and acceptance by the Church that we call him the real Author of the Bible. And we do not take this to be a contradiction. Rather we call it a mystery—similar to the mystery of Jesus, who while truly the Son of God is at the same time truly the Son of Man. Just so, each book of the Bible is truly authored by a human being, yet at the same time each book is authored by God himself.

The Church has declared to be the "canon" or accepted books of the Bible only those particular religious writings that it has experienced over a long period of time to be divinely inspired. The human character of each book is clearly evident in its origins and history. The inspired character of the Scriptures, however, is a truth of faith—something that makes sense only to those who believe in the God whose Word the Bible is.

# Part I
# The Old Testament

# Overview

## Exile and Homecoming

T he land of Canaan was the Promised Land for Israel. Yet the chosen people were displaced from their land on two occasions. After the patriarchs (usually considered the descendants of Abraham, primarily Isaac, Jacob and Joseph) had dwelt in the land, the descendants of Jacob found themselves enslaved in Egypt. Centuries later the people of Judah again found themselves exiled, this time to Babylon. Not surprisingly, the Jews in exile reflected on the earlier events of the Exodus and learned lessons that helped explain their current plight in Babylon. Twice God used the experience of separation from the land as an opportunity for his people to grow spiritually, and twice God mercifully returned his people to their land.

### Egypt and the Exodus

All of Israel's history was played out against the whirl of ancient international politics. Thus before studying the Old Testament it is helpful to get a sense of the broad outline of the history of the ancient Near East. Always bear in mind that many of the books in the Old Testament were written hundreds of years after the events they relate. Knowing what was happening to God's people at the time of the books' composition will help us better appreciate their message.

We can give only approximate dates for the generations of Israel's ancestors listed in Genesis. We are safe in saying, however, that Abraham and Sarah, Isaac and Rebekah, Jacob and his wives and his children and grandchildren lived between 2000 and 1550 B.C. God made a covenant in which he promised Abraham a large family whose descendants would inherit the land of Canaan. Joseph, one of Jacob's sons, was then sold into slavery in Egypt but rose to a position of power second only to the king, Pharaoh. When famine

---

drove Joseph's father and brothers to Egypt seeking food, they settled there for many generations.

When Joseph and his family arrived in Egypt, foreign invaders called the Hyksos were ruling the country. When the native Egyptians regained the throne, they enslaved those who had cooperated with the foreign regime—and this included the Hebrews. God then called Moses to lead the Hebrews back to Canaan, the land of Abraham, Isaac and Jacob. After a series of plagues, Pharaoh finally agreed to let the Hebrews leave. Later, when Pharaoh regretted this decision and sent his army to pursue the Hebrews, it seemed likely that the Hebrews would be recaptured and returned to slavery. God, however, intervened to assure the Hebrews' escape. The Exodus, as this escape is called, took place sometime in the mid-thirteenth century B.C. The annual celebration of Passover commemorates God's freeing his people.

## The Promised Land

God appeared to Moses at Mount Sinai, which is in the desert between Egypt and present-day Israel, and gave him the Ten Commandments, establishing another covenant with his people. The Exodus from Egypt and the Sinai Covenant formed the Hebrews into the nation Israel.

Moses and those of his generation who had come out of Egypt died during the forty years the Israelites remained in the wilderness of Sinai. Joshua then succeeded Moses as leader and led the Israelites into "the Promised Land," where initially they remained a loose federation of twelve tribes (descended from Jacob's sons). After Joshua, however, there was no single leader whom all twelve tribes acknowledged. But God eventually raised local leaders called *judges* who led one or more of the tribes against various enemies.

## Kingdoms of Judah and Israel

The Philistines, who had invaded and settled along the coast of Canaan, competed for territory with the tribes of Israel. As the Philistines pushed farther inland, they became a threat too big for local Israelite leaders to handle. Clearly Israel needed a king, so God inspired the priest and prophet Samuel to anoint Saul the first king of Israel. Although traditionalists opposed the establishment of a monarchy, kingly rule eventually was accepted as a necessity if the nation was to survive.

The books of Samuel (1 Samuel and 2 Samuel) describe the coming of the monarchy and the reigns of the first two kings, Saul and David. The books of Kings (1 Kings and 2 Kings) describe the rule of David's son Solomon and his building of the Temple in Jerusalem and the subsequent division of the kingdom into two realms. While the dynasty of David continued to rule the southern kingdom, called Judah, a series of short-lived dynasties ruled the less stable northern kingdom, called Israel. The books of Kings follow the story of the kingdoms to their ends. Israel eventually was destroyed by the Assyrian Empire in the late eighth century B.C. The Babylonians then conquered Judah in the early sixth century B.C. and destroyed the Temple in Jerusalem.

## Babylonian Exile

The books of Joshua, Judges, 1 Samuel and 2 Samuel and 1 Kings and 2 Kings were compiled during the Exile of the Jews in Babylon. God inspired the authors of these works to provide an answer to the Jews, who were perplexed by the destruction of the monarchy and the loss of their land. These books explain that unfaithfulness to the Sinai Covenant was the cause of the Jewish exiles' current situation. But the books also hold out the hope that renewal of covenant fidelity may bring God's mercy and the recovery of the land.

During the united monarchy, God inspired authors who wrote many of the texts later included in the books of Genesis, Exodus, Leviticus and Numbers. God also inspired authors from the separated northern kingdom to write other texts, later compiled into these books. And during the Exile, God inspired priests to compose other materials and to compile the books into the form we now have. These priestly authors encouraged the exiles to re-examine the meaning of the covenant and to renew themselves spiritually in light of its demands.

Throughout the monarchy, during the Exile, and beyond, God raised up spokesmen to proclaim his covenant message. These spokesmen, the prophets, challenged the people's lack of fidelity to

Yahweh, their God. When the destruction of the kingdoms brought the people near despair, the words of the prophets helped explain the cause of the disaster: The Exile was God's judgment on his unfaithful people.

## The Return

In 539 B.C., Cyrus of Persia conquered the Babylonian Empire and allowed the exiled Jews to return to their land. He also provided funds for the rebuilding of the Temple in Jerusalem. Although some of the refugees who returned the very next year immediately laid the foundations for a new Temple, they soon abandoned the project. In 520 B.C., when a second group returned, the work was resumed and construction of the Second Temple was completed in 515 B.C.

Judea remained a Persian province until Alexander the Great conquered Persia in the late fourth century B.C. Alexander was kind to the Jews, as were many of his successors. Then, in the second century B.C., control of Judea passed from one group of Alexander's successors to another. Unlike Alexander, the new rulers were often cruel to the Jews and tried to force them to abandon their religion and accept Greek ways.

The Book of Daniel tells of the struggles of Daniel and his friends during the Babylonian Exile. Because the author of the book knew that the Jews were once again in danger of being assimilated by a foreign culture, he encouraged his contemporaries to resist the demands of their Greek rulers. God had enabled Daniel to remain faithful to the covenant while in Babylon. The author of Daniel knew that God also would empower the Jews suffering persecution by the Greeks to remain faithful to him.

Eventually, the Maccabee family led the Jewish revolt against the Greeks, which resulted in an independent Jewish state that existed almost eighty years. In 63 B.C., however, the Romans took control of the region and incorporated the Jewish state into their empire.

## Naming God's People

At this point, we need to clarify certain terminology. What name should we apply to God's people? It depends on the period of time.

Abraham and his family, through their time in Egypt, are properly called *Hebrews*. The Exodus and the covenant at Mount Sinai form Abraham's descendants into a nation called *Israel*. Thus from the Exodus through the united monarchy the people are called *Israelites*. During the separate monarchies, the people are called by the name of their respective kingdoms, *Israel* or *Judah*. From the Exile onward, the people are called *Jews* and their religion is called *Judaism*. Both these terms derive from the kingdom name *Judah*.

There are, however, several uses of the name *Israel*. For example, it is an additional name bestowed upon the patriarch Jacob. Politically, *Israel* is also the name of the united monarchy, and after the division of the kingdom it is the name of the northern kingdom. The prophets often used the name "Israel" to signify the people's spiritual identity, without reference to any political division.

## Books of the Old Testament

We will usually employ the Jewish designations for what we Christians call the "Old Testament." The Jewish Scriptures have three major sections: the Torah, the Prophets and the Writings. The Torah (which means Law) is also called the Pentateuch (meaning "five scrolls"). The Torah includes Genesis, Exodus, Leviticus, Numbers and Deuteronomy. Next come the Prophets. The Former Prophets include the books of Joshua, Judges, 1 Samuel and 2 Samuel, and 1 Kings and 2 Kings. The Latter Prophets is divided into the three major prophets (Isaiah, Jeremiah and Ezekiel) and the twelve "minor" prophets (referring not to their importance but to the size of their recorded preaching). In the Jewish Scriptures, the Book of Daniel is not included in the prophets. Daniel is grouped with all the remaining books, called the Writings.

# Genesis 1

## How God Intended
## Creation to Be

W e humans find stories very appealing. Psychology tells us that stories are subconscious mirrors of life, reflecting back to us images of our own undigested experience. By getting into a story we tap into our own inner selves.

Because God is the best of teachers, it should come as no surprise that the Bible is full of all kinds of stories. Some are imaginative inventions, such as the story of Jonah and the parables in the Gospels. Some stories are more historical, as in the books of 1 Kings and 2 Kings, which even suggest where the reader might find more information. (Regrettably, these other documents have not survived the centuries.) Still other stories are a cross between real events and creative embellishment.

### Genesis Chronology

Because we find the creation account at the very beginning of the Bible, we might assume that it is the oldest of all scriptural material. Actually, the first eleven chapters of Genesis are of relatively late origin. This material was added to serve as an introduction to the Torah (Pentateuch) in the late fifth century B.C., when various traditions were being knitted together into the unified whole we read in our Bibles today. The compilers of the early chapters of Genesis wanted to preface the Scriptures with an overarching statement about their faith in Yahweh, the God of Israel, and about prehistory—the time before Abraham. Over the centuries, the faith of the Jews had matured, and around 500 B.C., in the period after the Babylonian Exile, that faith recognized Yahweh as not only the God of Israel but as *the one and only* God. Genesis proclaims that since the beginning of time Yahweh alone is God. The universe is entirely his making and his domain. Understandably, these foundational truths properly belong at the very head of salvation history.

The first eleven chapters of Genesis are the result of this line of thinking. Blending oral and written traditions from both pagan and Jewish sources, the authors of the creation account in Genesis 1:1–2:4a make a ringing proclamation of Israel's faith at the height of its maturity. They uncompromisingly affirm that God is one, that he is the creator of all, that he is all good, and that his intentions for the human race are the most wonderful imaginable.

## The Creation Story

The framework of the creation story in Genesis includes both an ancient concept of the cosmos as well as Jewish reverence for the Sabbath. God is portrayed in the manner of a carpenter doing a week's work. At the close of each day, he steps back to admire his handiwork and is especially pleased with the final product—human beings, both male and female—on the sixth day. He then observes the Sabbath and rests.

The ancient concept of the cosmos positions the earth at the center of the universe, with the sun, moon and stars moving in an arc across the sky. Today we realize that while the moon does indeed revolve around the earth, the earth and other planets revolve around the sun. We also know that our sun is but one of billions of stars in our Milky Way galaxy. Does this mean the creation story that begins Genesis—and thus introduces the entire Bible—is wrong or untrue or at least unreliable?

## The Story and Its Meaning

The creation account is in the form of a story, thus arguments about whether the earth was made in exactly six days and whether evolution opposes the Bible are not the point. The authors of Genesis were not providing a scientific explanation of the origins of the cosmos. They were telling a story.

But what is the meaning of their story? What truth does it have to offer us today? Now we are at the heart of the matter, where we find a set of much more relevant questions: What has God revealed to humankind in this particular part of the Scriptures? What are we believers in God's Word asked to accept here, and what faith enlightenment are we offered?

The details of the story are not the issue; the meaning of the story is what is relevant for us today. For believing Jews and Christians, the story of creation is God's own revelation of himself and of his relationship to the cosmos, which he sustains in existence. We discover in this story that God is good, that he is intimately involved in his creation, and that his will for humanity is marvelously gracious.

# Genesis 2–11

## What Went Wrong?

By the time we reach Genesis 12 in the Bible, we encounter Abraham, a real man who lived approximately four thousand years ago. But the human race had been around for millions of years before the people and events detailed in "history" or the Bible.

To help us better understand the chronology involved here, suppose all of human existence were to be scaled along the 100-yard length of a football field. All of human existence before Abraham would fill ninety-nine yards, two feet and nine inches. Only the last *three inches* of the field would be the time from Abraham to our present day!

With this perspective, we can appreciate what the authors of Genesis were up against when they asked themselves "What happened before Abraham?" Within their own oral and written tradition there was little to shed light on this question. When they searched elsewhere they did come up with a few scattered materials. Mesopotamian writings, for example, contained genealogies reaching back before 2000 B.C. Sumerian literature told of a worldwide flood in primeval times during which a hero escaped by building an ark and taking aboard with him the seed of all living things.

### Constructing Prehistory

Borrowing freely from such materials, the sacred writers of Genesis constructed an outline of prehistory: creation; the first humans and the origin of evil; the great Flood; and the development of different peoples and tongues. The sacred writers did not take their adopted source material at face value, however. They simply rid it of anything contrary to faith in Yahweh. (We will see examples of this when we examine the story of the Flood.) The authors then used the purified material as a framework for explaining prehistory, whatever its actual content. The vehicle for this explanation is the symbolism of the stories found in Genesis 1–4 (the fortunes of Adam and Eve), Genesis 5–9 (Noah and the Flood), and Genesis 11 (the Tower of Babel).

## The Fortunes of Adam and Eve

The six-day creation story ends on a happy note of harmony between God and humans. But then something went wrong. Chapters 2 through 11 of Genesis teach that all disharmony in creation is the fault of humans. The stories of these chapters show an ever-increasing downward spiral of sinfulness, in which as sin increases the human life span decreases.

The purpose and value of the Adam and Eve story lie in its meaning, not in its surface details. The meaning has to do with the nature of human beings and the universal problem of evil. Strong and unequivocal stands are taken on these issues—stands still accepted as foundational for Jewish and Christian faith today.

In Hebrew, *Adam* means "the man" and *Eve* means "origin of life." In Hebrew, these names function like the title of the medieval morality play *Everyman*, in which all persons are supposed to see themselves literally mirrored in the central character. The story emphasizes our glory as human beings. We—human beings—are creation's climax. Humans alone are "very good" and made in God's own image.

But there is a dark side to the story. The natural state of friendship that humans are designed to have with God, a friendship symbolized by Adam and Eve living in God's garden, has been disrupted. God, however, is not the *cause* of the disorder we now experience within creation and within ourselves. The disorder is of our own doing. Adam and Eve sinned by disobeying God. Likewise, every person's sin is fundamentally a disobeying of God's law, a law intended to promote authentic human living. By sinning, we oppose our humanity, striving to "be like God" (Genesis 3:5).

Weaving together available tales of "origins," the Genesis writers created something distinctively new in order to profess profound beliefs. Unlike other religions of the day, Judaism refused to take the easy way out by explaining the problem of evil as the fault of the gods. Without the slightest compromise, the authors of Genesis insist that Yahweh is all good and that evil must be explained as a malfunction of creation itself, apart from God.

## Noah and the Flood

The Noah story provides a grounding for the universal outlook the Jewish faith had acquired by the year 500 B.C. when Genesis 1–11 was written. Yahweh is no longer regarded as the private God of Israel; he is the God of humankind as a whole. Nor is it Yahweh's intention to save only the Jews; God's salvation is intended for all people, although it will be accomplished through Israel.

The authors of Genesis purify the Sumerian flood story of things contrary to their faith. The Flood is God's just punishment of sin, not a peevish act of the gods who considered human noise intolerable. Noah remains a mortal man, unlike his Sumerian counterpart, who becomes immortal. Thus, the purified narrative teaches God's concern for all humankind. After the Flood, God makes the first salvation covenant with Noah (see Genesis 8:20–22), through which all Noah's descendants will benefit. While Abraham and the Jewish race are descended from one of Noah's sons, they are not to forget that they are related by blood to all nations.

## The Tower of Babel

Despite God's covenant with Noah, the human inclination to sin continues—disrupting our relationship with God, our relationships with other individuals, and the relationships of nations with one another. The skillful authors use narrative details to teach the havoc caused by sin. In chapter 3, the first sin causes the humans to be aware of their nakedness. They hide from God and put on clothing for the first time. Sin has disrupted the easy and open relationship they enjoyed with God and with one another.

The sin of the first humans was an attempt to "be like God" (3:5). When we reach chapter 11, we find another form of the same sin. The peoples of the earth decide to build a tower to reach to heaven: "Come, let us build ourselves a city, and a tower with its top in the heavens, and let us make a name for ourselves; otherwise we shall be scattered abroad upon the face of the whole earth" (11:4).

Ironically, that which the people had feared is the very effect their actions produce. The authors use the fact that humans speak different languages and cannot always communicate with one another as yet another sign of the damage sin has done.

The biblical stage is set for the appearance of Abraham.

# Abraham

## The First Believer

Every nation has its heroes—men and women who serve as rallying points for the people's sense of identity and destiny. European countries have their kings, queens and generals. The United States of America has George Washington and Abraham Lincoln.

National heroes are legendary in more than one sense. Not only is their actual history revered but legends grow up around them, enhancing their image. Such is the legend of the young George Washington chopping down a cherry tree and refusing to lie to his father about it.

Ancient Israel had two such heroes: Abraham and Moses. Both lived before exact historical records were kept. Both lived keenly in memory, however, because of their central roles in Israel's identity as a nation and in Israel's vision of her future. Both were the objects of legends that underscored their greatness.

### The Abraham Tradition

Because Abraham was by far the more remote of the two heroes of Hebrew faith, legend figures even more prominently in the biblical narrative about him (see Genesis 11:27–25:10). Generous allowance must be made for the fact that Abraham lived a thousand years before any known documents about him were written. Also, as found in the Bible, the Abraham traditions are filtered through faith understandings that resulted from the Exodus. Thus Abraham is treated in hindsight fashion as one who prefigures the greatest event in Israel's history.

Still, the Abraham narratives cannot be taken lightly. There is not the least doubt that in the history of Israel this man was singularly important. The legends that grew up around him and are preserved in the Bible add to the core of factual accounts by making clear what kind of man Abraham was and how God gave him a foundational role in salvation history.

Abraham lived around the beginning of the second millennium B.C. He was born in the ancient city of Ur, located in the southeast corner of modern Iraq. Ur was at the lower eastern extremity of the Fertile Crescent, an arc of land stretching along the northern edge of the Arabian Desert. In Abraham's day the settlement of Haran to the north marked the center of the Fertile Crescent. From Haran, the crescent bent to the southwest, ending in the land of Canaan, which would later be called—at various times in history—Judea, Palestine and Israel.

Abraham (Abram) married Sarah (Sarai), and the couple migrated to Haran with Abraham's father. Later the couple moved into Canaan, eventually settling at Mamre. Their son Isaac married Rebekah, who bore Jacob, also called "Israel," and Jacob's sons became known as the founders of the twelve tribes of Israel. Joseph, the favored son of Jacob, brought about the settlement of the entire clan in Egypt, where they were saved from starvation and where things went well for Jacob's offspring for a long time. The second half of the Book of Genesis describes the fortunes of Abraham's family through these several generations.

## What Do We Believe about Abraham?

As the Word of God, the Book of Genesis tells us a great deal about the foundations of the faith we profess today. Even where legend is the vehicle, the biblical text remains divine revelation all the same. We should therefore address the question: What is the Book of Genesis asking us to believe about Abraham?

Abraham is God's chosen instrument to create the foundations for the Exodus, an event that will have deep religious meaning for all humankind. The Genesis narrative unfolds this theme in three parts. First, Abraham experiences the call of the God of Israel, Yahweh. Second, Abraham enters into a solemn pact, or covenant, with Yahweh. Third, to the very end Abraham remains faithful to Yahweh's call and covenant—meaning that Yahweh will fulfill the awesome promises he made to Abraham.

The account of Abraham's call by Yahweh is found in chapter 12 of Genesis: "Now the Lord said to Abram, 'Go from your country and your kindred and your father's house to the land that I will show you. I will make of you a great nation, and I will bless you, and make your name great, so that you will be a blessing'" (12:1–2). The statement leaves much unsaid. For example, Abraham had no means of knowing who this deity was; the identification "Yahweh" was first revealed to Moses. (In Genesis, the use of the name Yahweh is a deliberate later insertion.) What's more, polytheism dominated the religious understanding of Abraham's time. Partial and ambiguous as Abraham's experience of the true God may have been, however, it was enough to challenge and win his faith. He responded by believing; Genesis suggests that is what made all the difference.

## The Abrahamic Covenant

Chapter 15 of Genesis tells of the covenant between Yahweh and Abraham. Covenants were a normal part of life in ancient times. They were used primarily to seal agreements of special importance between two parties. Among people who could not read or write and who were continually on the move, a covenant had the same force and meaning as our written contracts today. An exchange of promises was solemnized by sacrificing an animal and calling the gods to witness. A shared meal might follow, signifying oneness in life and mutual dependency with regard to the covenant promises.

Abraham's part of the covenant agreement with Yahweh is taken for granted. Nothing deters him from remaining true to Yahweh, and he is resolved that nothing will. The problem seems to be with Yahweh's end of the bargain. Assured at Haran that he would become the father of a great nation and be mightily blessed, Abraham is now aging and is still waiting for God's promise to materialize. He presents his difficulty to Yahweh, who first tells him to count the stars if he can, then adds, "So shall your descendants be" (15:5).

At this point Yahweh initiates a formal covenant and instructs Abraham to prepare animals for sacrifice. Abraham obeys, then waits for Yahweh to complete the covenant ceremony. But hours pass. Finally, when darkness settles, God makes his move: "When the sun had gone down and it was dark, a smoking fire-pot and a flaming torch passed between these pieces [of animals]. On that day the

Lord made a covenant with Abram, saying, 'To your descendants I give this land, from the river of Egypt to the great river, the river Euphrates'" (15:17–18).

Like the covenant with Noah, this covenant prefigures the great covenant to come during the Exodus, at the hands of Moses on Mount Sinai. The God of Abraham, Isaac and Jacob will then covenant with the entire people of Israel. More immediately, God reassures Abraham in the strongest possible way that he is faithful to his word and that the original promise he made to Abraham would indeed be brought to pass.

### Abraham in Salvation History

Finally, Genesis relates that against staggering odds Abraham remains completely faithful to Yahweh to the very end. He grows very old, as does his wife, Sarah, before the birth of Isaac, their first and only "child of the promise." But the greatest test of faith is still to come. Chapter 22 of Genesis tells how God instructs Abraham to prepare his young son for sacrifice, staying his hand only at the last possible moment.

On balance, Abraham's enduring place in salvation history hinges most of all on this aspect of the Genesis narrative: Of all God's people, Abraham had the least tangible evidence for Yahweh's fidelity or power to keep his word. Yet no one adhered to God more tenaciously than he did. Not only was Abraham the first to believe in the true God; the intensity of his faith places him first among all believers.

The remaining chapters of Genesis trace the giving of the promise to successive generations of Abraham's family. God does not follow human ways. In continuing the covenant, God is sovereign. Yahweh repeatedly chooses not the first-born son but another to receive the covenant promises. God chose Isaac over his older brother, Ishmael; Jacob over his elder sibling, Esau; and Judah over three older brothers.

The Book of Genesis closes with the descendants of Abraham in Egypt, safe from starvation. But much history passes unmentioned between the end of Genesis and the beginning of Exodus. During the generations after Jacob, a dynastic change in Egypt resulted in the enslavement of the Israelites, taking them from prosperity to slavery.

# Moses

## The Exodus and the Wilderness

If we can speak of peaks and valleys in history, the Exodus was more than a peak for Israel. It was Mount Everest. All previous history was viewed as leading up to the Exodus and all succeeding history as flowing from it. So immense was this event in Israel's eyes that it has remained an inexhaustible source of religious renewal for thousands of years.

### Historically and Biblically

The historical facts are simple. Toward the middle of the thirteenth century B.C., the reigning pharaoh of Egypt released the enslaved Hebrews. Under the leadership of a man named Moses, the Hebrews left the capital city of Rameses, crossed a body of water to the north of the Gulf of Suez, and headed south along the western coast of the Sinai Peninsula. After wandering for many years and overcoming famine, drought and periodic attacks by marauding bands, the Hebrews eventually headed north again, this time along the eastern side of the Sinai Peninsula. They passed the Dead Sea on the east, crossed the Jordan River, and entered the land of Canaan after the death of Moses. For many years they battled the inhabitants of the land, eventually supplanting them and settling there.

The biblical account of these facts is far richer and more detailed. The books of Exodus, Leviticus, Numbers and Deuteronomy carry the story through the wilderness wanderings. The Book of Joshua (which we explore in the next chapter) completes the story by picking it up after Moses' death and covering the entry into Canaan. Although the biblical account examines the journey for the sake of telling the history, the inspired authors were more interested in examining the relationship between God and his covenant people.

The narrative of this story unfolds in a halting manner, with lengthy digressions constantly interrupting the sequence of events. As we have inherited them, these particular Scriptures are a blending of two concerns: the traditional Exodus story itself and a sanctioning of religious practices that grew up afterward. By placing the origin of religious practices within the context of the Exodus event, the biblical authors emphasize the divine character of these practices in the strongest way possible.

Christian readers often find the non-narrative material of little practical interest. Although the lengthy accounts of dietary laws, purification rituals and liturgical rubrics seem a curiosity, this material actually illustrates why Judaism calls the first five books of the Bible the "Torah," or "Law." Jewish understanding sees nothing legalistic or negative in the term *law* as used here. Rather the Torah is God's gracious gift to believers, illuminating the natural shoals and pitfalls of human existence so that life can be embraced to the full and pursued in happiness. The author of Deuteronomy says of observing the Law: "This is no trifling matter for you, but rather your very life; through it you may live long in the land that you are crossing over the Jordan to possess" (32:47).

## The Sinai Covenant

If the Exodus event as a whole was a kind of Mount Everest, the peak of the mountain was the Sinai Covenant (see Exodus 19–24). Before Sinai, the Hebrews had only a vague relationship with the God of Abraham, Isaac and Jacob. Ever afterward, however, they were the people of Yahweh, bound to him by defined creed, religious practice and morality.

We have seen that a covenant was a solemn pact between two parties. In the Sinai Covenant the entire Hebrew people enter into an agreement with Yahweh. For his part, Yahweh pledges to lead the Hebrews safely into the Promised Land of Canaan: "If you obey my voice and keep my covenant, you shall be my treasured possession out of all the peoples. Indeed, the whole earth is mine, but you shall be for me a priestly kingdom and a holy nation" (Exodus 19:5–6). In response, Israel pledges obedience to God's commandments: "The people all answered as one: 'Everything that the Lord has spoken we will do'" (Exodus 19:8).

To ratify the covenant Moses builds an altar with twelve stones, representing the twelve tribes of Israel (see Exodus 24:4). He instructs that young bulls be slain in sacrifice to Yahweh and that their blood be gathered in containers. Part of the blood is then poured on the altar and part is sprinkled on the people. The Hebrews know that as blood is poured out from anything living, life flows out as well. Blood stands for life itself. The altar is God's table; whatever is placed on it belongs to God. The blood poured on the altar is given over to God, becoming a symbol of his own life. Being sprinkled with this blood means being joined to God.

## One Central Truth

The greatness of Moses is beyond question. He was a man of unparalleled holiness, wisdom and courage. Yet as in the case of the Exodus narratives as a whole the writers use a good deal of creativity to get across their central affirmation. For example, the story of Moses' escape from death as an infant (see Exodus 2) has parallels in other literature of the time. To signal the future greatness of their subject, ancient writers often would tell of a miraculous rescue from death during the person's infancy.

Once again we must distinguish between the central truth that the biblical writer affirms and the means the writer employs to convey that truth. Throughout the Exodus narratives the central truth is clear—God himself planned and brought about the Exodus. He was intimately and directly involved in the unfolding of the Exodus, for it was the keystone of his plan of salvation for humankind.

The literary forms used to state this truth, however, are varied. The biblical text before us today is a patchwork of individual stories, traditions and religious laws. Even the "eyewitness" nature of the text is clearly a literary device; internal textual evidence makes it clear that the material was composed long after the events took place.

Thus to correctly understand God's Word we need to make a distinction between the revealed message and the human form of the text. Consider, for example, Deuteronomy 20:10–14, where God instructs the Israelites on procedures to be followed in capturing towns. If the people surrender peacefully, God directs, then they are merely to be enslaved. But if they resist, all men are to be executed and women and children are to be taken as "booty." Here God's Word seems to be hopelessly in conflict with itself—these instructions do not seem to fit with the image of the compassionate God revealed in Genesis or the pages of the New Testament.

We are reminded again that the Bible was written in a thoroughly human way. The author of this passage rightly believes that Yahweh was behind Israel's settlement in Canaan—and this is the truth the writer is affirming. But to make this truth concrete, the author uses the literary device of anthropomorphism. God is portrayed as a field commander telling the Israelites how to conduct their warfare, even to the point of carrying out barbarous practices that were standard at the time.

The most important thing for us to remember today is that divine revelation unfolded one step at a time. The Israelites were permitted to prevail against the Canaanites so that eventually the entire human race might come to terms with God's will for peace among all nations.

## Reading Guidelines

Here are some suggestions for reading these particular books of the Bible: The narrative portion breaks off after Exodus 24 and resumes at Numbers 10:11. Be sure to note the story in Numbers 13–14; it explains from a theological perspective the reason for the forty years of wandering in the wilderness. Logically, the Book of Numbers should end with an account of the death of Moses, but because Deuteronomy follows Numbers and is basically a long sermon by Moses, the account of Moses' death is postponed until the end of Deuteronomy.

Chapter 19 of Leviticus is well worth reading. Some of the material deals with laws of ritual purity, which need not concern us. But many elements of this reading can provide an interesting examination of conscience. Verse 13, for example, speaks of justice in handling wages. Verse 14 reads: "You shall not revile the deaf or put a stumbling block before the blind." Verse 18 is the great commandment (later repeated by Jesus): "You shall love your neighbor as yourself."

# The Former Prophets

## Joshua, Judges, 1 Samuel and 2 Samuel, 1 Kings and 2 Kings

The Book of Deuteronomy and the books of the Deuteronomic History (Joshua, Judges, 1 Samuel and 2 Samuel, and 1 Kings and 2 Kings) were written seven centuries after the events they describe, in connection with the Babylonian Exile. (A nucleus of Deuteronomy, namely chapters 12–26, may have existed earlier and is often referred to as the "Book of the Covenant," which inspired King Josiah's reforms described in 2 Kings 23.) The books of the Former Prophets are prophetic in the sense that they helped Israel understand the causes of the Exile. Moses' call to covenant fidelity in Deuteronomy stands in marked contrast to the reality the later books describe. Israel was unfaithful to the covenant—and lost the land.

At the time of the Exile, Israel's hopes for the future depended on reviving a sense of "divine destiny" to control the land of Canaan. The biblical scribes used the memory of Israel's first possession of the land to bolster her resolve to repossess it.

### Joshua

In the book of Joshua, the accounts of the Israelites' entry into the Promised Land are simplified and romanticized. Because Canaan was at the lower west end of the Fertile Crescent, it was the only land corridor for travel, commerce and the waging of war between Egypt and other large nations—especially Babylonia and Assyria. Ownership of this land had been a constant bone of contention well before biblical times and continued with the occupation led by Joshua.

When the Israelites began their takeover, Canaan officially belonged to Egypt. At that time, however, Egypt became embroiled with internal problems, losing the will and the resources to hold

Canaan. What's more, the Israelites were not the only ones contesting for this land. From the areas of Greece and the Balkans came the "sea peoples," known in the Bible as the "Philistines."

The Canaanites were a farming people. They lived in fortified cities close to their farmland and had no national government and no armies. It is hard to be sure just how great a threat the Hebrews first posed, for in contrast to the Canaanites the Israelites were nomadic sheepherders. Eventually, however, and not without frequent warfare, the Israelites and the Philistines supplanted the Canaanites.

## Judges

The highly idealized story of the Israelites' settlement of the Promised Land as found in the Book of Joshua gives way to the Book of Judges. The name comes from the heroes or "judges" who are featured in the narration of Israel's eventual success in securing a home in Canaan. In this patriarchal society it was customary for a father or grandfather to settle family disputes in the presence of the entire clan; thus he acted as "judge." By extension, one who exercised leadership for an entire tribe was called a *judge*.

The author of the Book of Judges is clearly more interested in theology than in history. Covering about two centuries (ca. 1200 to 1000 B.C.), the book paves the way for Israel's "golden age," the monarchies of David and Solomon. An underlying theme of the book is Israel's growing recognition through painful experience of the need for political unity among the twelve tribes. We see how the Israelites' initial attempts to settle Canaan by tribe, each faring for itself, eventually proved ineffective.

An equally important theme of the Book of Judges, repeated in cyclic fashion, is that Israel's well-being closely depends on fidelity to the Sinai Covenant. Each segment of the narrative follows the same pattern: A tribe's falling away from the covenant leads to oppression by enemies; repentance follows; and then divine liberation comes at the hands of judges, such as Deborah, Gideon and Samson. The final chapters of the book describe a civil war among the tribes, and the book ends with the pathetic note, "In those days there was no king in Israel; all the people did what was right in their own eyes" (21:25); some translations render this, "Each person did what he thought best." It was clearly time for a monarchy.

## 1 Samuel and 2 Samuel

The books of Samuel and Kings (each is a single book in the Hebrew Scriptures, but they are divided into two books each in Christian Bibles) narrate Israel's history from the end of the period of the judges (late eleventh century B.C.) until the Babylonian Exile, which began in 587 B.C. The books of Samuel center around the historic prophet of the same name, who appeared toward the close of the period of the judges and ushered Israel into the monarchies of Saul and David. In the form in which they come to us the books are an obvious compilation of different source materials. For example, there are two conflicting versions of Samuel's role in the establishment of the kingdom under Saul. 1 Samuel 10:1–6 is a pro-royalist account, showing Samuel eager to have the tribes united under a king. Immediately following, an anti-royalist account in 10:17–21 portrays Samuel berating the Israelites for wanting a human king in place of Yahweh. Both accounts are preserved in lasting tension with each other—one account telling what the monarchy could and should have been, the other telling the sad reality of how the monarchy led Israel astray.

King David holds center stage from chapter 16 of 1 Samuel until the close of 2 Samuel. He was clearly the focal point of Israel's hopes for the restoration of the kingdom ever after. The scribes who assembled these Scriptures—some four hundred years after David—were passionately committed to the resurrection of Israel's lost dynasty. They arranged their materials to tell how David had the sure formula for Israel's endurance as a kingdom: fidelity to the Sinai Covenant. King Solomon and his successors, however, compromised this formula, and tragic results followed. The lesson was clear: If after the Babylonian Exile Israel were to reconvert to Yahweh, the heyday of national independence experienced under David would return under his successor.

Thus we have an idealized history of David in 1 Samuel and 2 Samuel. The spirit of the Lord is upon him from the moment of his anointing at Samuel's hand (see 1 Samuel 16:1–13). After he crushes the Philistines and unifies the tribes as Saul could not, David strategically chooses a neutral site between the northern and southern tribes as his capital: Jerusalem. The Ark of the Covenant, the portable chest containing relics of the Exodus, is housed next to his palace, becoming the rallying point for a national religious revival. David reputedly plays the lyre at liturgical celebrations. He also sets up a centralized administrative system, which Solomon is to consolidate and use skillfully.

## 1 Kings and 2 Kings

1 Kings and 2 Kings start with the final days of David and end with the Babylonian invasion and conquest of Judah. Solomon builds the Temple in Jerusalem to house the Ark and centralizes all of Israel's worship there. Although Israel prospers under Solomon, his imposition of heavy taxes and forced labor on his people, especially the northern tribes, contains the seeds for the dissolution of the unified monarchy. After Solomon's son Rehoboam foolishly announces his intention to continue his father's policies and even make them more burdensome, the northern tribes reject his rule and form a separate kingdom. What's more, Solomon violates the Sinai Covenant by having hundreds of wives and concubines. In his later years (see 1 Kings 11), Solomon's wives lead him into worship of pagan idols. Eventually God sends a little-known prophet, Ahijah the Shilonite, to dramatically pronounce judgment on Solomon's ways and to decree the divine sanction of the division of the kingdom (see 11:29–39).

Active in the northern kingdom (Israel) sometime between 870 and 740 B.C. are two better-known prophets, Elijah and Elisha, who dominate the narrative in 1 Kings 17 through 2 Kings 13. The kings of the period exploited the poor, maintained their thrones by murder and terrorism, and favored the Canaanite god Baal over Yahweh. The notorious Jezebel was queen during this same period. Elijah and Elisha struggled tirelessly against these corruptions, achieving much success.

In literary form the narratives of Elijah and Elisha are highly dramatized. The miracle stories have an artistic flair; they are suspenseful and stark in their simplicity. For example, in 1 Kings 18,

Elijah single-handedly challenges four hundred prophets of Baal and with magnificent poise does them all in at once! In this account we are dealing with imaginative additions to history in order to make its meaning clearer. Yahweh unquestionably works through Elijah and Elisha for the ultimate good of his people—and the miracle stories brilliantly highlight this truth of faith.

Despite the teaching of these prophets, however, and that of Isaiah, Jeremiah, Ezekiel and some of the other prophets we will examine in the next chapters, the kingdoms of Israel and Judah continued on their faithless ways, rendering them too weak to withstand outside pressure. Assyria eventually destroyed Israel in 721 B.C.; Babylonia, having conquered Assyria, destroyed Judah in 587 B.C.

Politics and armies could not save the tiny kingdoms. Only fidelity to Yahweh could have enabled the kingdoms to survive, but it was not to be. The many sins of Israel's leaders and the particularly heinous crimes of King Manasseh of Judah were the reasons for the coming of God's judgment in the form of foreign armies. (See 2 Kings 17:7–21 for the reason Israel fell and 2 Kings 21:10–16 for the cause of Yahweh's judgment against Judah.)

According to the writers of the books of the Former Prophets, destruction was the inevitable price Israel and Judah had to pay for not holding to the Sinai Covenant. In God's mercy, however, destruction was not the final word of the story.

# The Latter Prophets

## Isaiah, Jeremiah and Ezekiel

In the original Greek, the term *prophet* is a combination of *pro* and *phetes*. *Pro* means "on behalf of," and *phetes* means "speaker." The root meaning of *prophet* is "someone who speaks on behalf of someone else." Thus the biblical prophet was a person who spoke on behalf of God with God's own authority. The primary role of a prophet was to confront Israel with her failings to live up to the Sinai Covenant and to warn of judgment, which could be averted only by repentance and renewal.

To situate the prophets historically we start with Samuel at the close of the period of the judges (late eleventh century B.C.) and continue almost without interruption into the era that follows Israel's return from the Babylonian Exile in 538 B.C. In a larger sense, Moses was the first to exercise the prophetic role; Joshua and judges, such as Deborah, did this as well. Yet the role of prophet was first formally recognized with Samuel, although by using hindsight the author of Deuteronomy calls Moses a prophet (see 34:10).

Prophets were not ordained, as the priests were, and they held no official role within the religious establishment. They acted on their own, out of conviction that Yahweh had called them and sent them to speak his word. For this reason the prophets frequently met with disbelief and were treated badly—and small wonder. Not only did they have harsh things to say to their hearers; they also easily rubbed official religious leaders the wrong way, implying that they were failing in their job. Although some prophets such as Samuel managed to win credibility and were then accepted without question, others were recognized as prophets only after they were dead and gone.

### Isaiah

Two major prophets of Israel are Isaiah and Jeremiah, both of whom lived in Judah, the southern kingdom. Isaiah lived in the eighth century B.C. while the northern kingdom suffered extinction. The preaching of this prophet, sometimes called "Isaiah of Jerusalem" or "First Isaiah," is found in chapters 1 through 39 of the Book of Isaiah.

Isaiah began preaching in the year King Uzziah of Judah died (742 B.C.) and continued through the reigns of Jotham, Ahaz and Hezekiah of Judah. Combining profound personal holiness with a calm, majestic vision of Yahweh's goodness and fidelity to his people, Isaiah addressed his preaching to a weak and vacillating King Ahaz. Isaiah bade the king and his troubled contemporaries to rely on religious conversion and loyalty to the Sinai Covenant rather than on political action. Even while condemning immoral behavior and threatening divine punishment, Isaiah was tempered by a peace-filled confidence in the power of Yahweh to make all things come out well for Judah in the end.

Regrettably, Isaiah's message fell on deaf ears. Threatened by invasion from neighboring kingdoms, King Ahaz turned his back on Yahweh's power and instead sought an alliance with the Assyrian Empire. This shortsighted "solution" increased Judah's indebtedness to Assyria and allowed greater penetration of Assyria's pagan gods into the worship life of Judah.

Isaiah's written legacy continued by proxy, so to speak, through a school of disciples who prophesied to new situations as they believed Isaiah himself would have done. Chapters 40 through 55 of the Book of Isaiah are the preaching of a disciple or disciples during the Babylonian Exile. The message of "Second Isaiah" encouraged the exiles to believe that God would bring them back to their homeland in a mighty action like the great Exodus of old.

Chapters 56 through 66 come from the time after the return to the land. The so-called "Third Isaiah" preached in the earliest years after the return of the exiles, roughly 538–520 B.C. His message is one of encouragement and hope for a people who might easily succumb to depression and despair as they faced the hardships involved with rebuilding their homeland. The book of the prophet Zechariah also reflects the preaching of prophets from different periods. Indeed all the books of the prophets were edited to a greater or lesser degree to update their messages in the light of new situations facing God's people.

## Jeremiah

The Book of Jeremiah gives us many personal details about him, making him perhaps the most attractive personality among the prophets. It was Jeremiah's unenviable task to tell Judah (late seventh and early sixth centuries) that all hope was lost in the face of the mounting peril from Babylonia and to urge the people to come to terms while they still were able. Only with the greatest reluctance did Jeremiah accept Yahweh's call, so inadequate did he feel and so apprehensive was he of failure (see Jeremiah 1:1–10). His worst fears were fulfilled. He was derided by self-appointed prophets who gave Judah the false assurance that all was well. Scorned by the people and imprisoned as a troublemaker, Jeremiah complained to Yahweh and tried to back out of his mission without success (see Jeremiah 20:7–9). In the end Jeremiah succeeded in preparing Judah for its religious rebirth during the Babylonian captivity. Jeremiah was confident that God would yet renew the covenant, a covenant that would be written not on tablets of stone but in the very hearts of God's people (see Jeremiah 31:33).

## Ezekiel

The prophet Ezekiel preached to his fellow exiles in Babylon. First, Ezekiel had to convince the original deportees that being uprooted from their homeland was not some temporary political misadventure. He had to confront the false hope that accompanied the first exiles in 597 B.C.: that is, the fact that the Temple still stood did not mean their captivity would be short-lived. Ezekiel also had to convince the exiles that what was befalling them and their nation was God's judgment upon their sinful ways. Ten years later, when the second wave of deportees brought the news that Jerusalem and its Temple were in fact destroyed, Ezekiel had to switch from words of judgment to words of hope, lest the exiles plummet from false hopes to bitter despair.

In chapter 34, we hear Ezekiel's promise that God himself would become the shepherd who would rescue his sheep. Ezekiel looked forward to a reunification of Israel and Judah, offering his most powerful image of hope for restoration by using the vision of the valley of dry bones (see chapter 37). In chapters 38 and 39, Ezekiel uses apocalyptic language (more on this literary form in a later chapter) to express God's victory and Israel's vindication.

The books of the prophets remain God's living Word to all ages. Today they are especially powerful as they speak to us of the folly of sin, especially in its corporate and communal dimension. We can take no comfort in the fact that everyone else seems to be living in the same way or that we are only following the crowd. Indeed the biblical prophets cry out to us across time, demanding that we see sin for what it really is and that we repent and be converted to God.

# The Minor Latter Prophets

## The Book of the Twelve

God bestowed the prophetic ministry on many lesser-known individuals. Compared to Isaiah, Jeremiah and Ezekiel, little or nothing is known about most of these other servants of the Lord. The Holy Spirit, who inspired these men to preach, also inspired generations in Israel to recognize their preaching as the Word of God. Their inspired words join those of Isaiah, Jeremiah and Ezekiel in calling God's people of every generation to serve him faithfully.

### Assyrian Dominance: The Final Years of Israel

Amos prophesied sometime from 760 to 750 B.C., a period of great prosperity during the lengthy reigns of Uzziah of Judah (783–742 B.C.) and Jeroboam II of Israel (786–746 B.C.). Amos was from the small southern town of Tekoa and worked as a shepherd. In chapters 1 and 2, we hear the prophet's oracles against the nations of the region: Damascus, Gaza, Tyre, Edom, Ammon, Moab, Judah and Israel. The most severe judgment is given to the northern kingdom Israel, however, where the wealthy were abusive to the poor: "They sell the righteous for silver, and the needy for a pair of sandals—they who trample the head of the poor into the dust of the earth, and push the afflicted out of the way" (2:6–7).

This time of great prosperity also was a time of great injustice. The rich became richer at the expense of the poor and the "houses of ivory" (3:15) of the ruling class were maintained on the back-breaking labor of the poor. In brutally frank terms, Amos denounced the wives of the aristocracy: "Hear this word, you cows of Bashan who are on Mount Samaria, who oppress the poor, who crush the needy, who say to their husbands, 'Bring us something to drink!' The Lord God has sworn by his holiness: The time is definitely coming when they will take you away with hooks, even the last of you with fishhooks" (4:1–2).

Amos insisted that simply going through the motions of worship while not practicing love of neighbor would not suffice. He offered a path of salvation to the northern kingdom: "Hate evil and love good, and establish justice in the gate; it may be that the Lord, the God of hosts, will be gracious to the remnant of Joseph [the northern tribes]" (5:15). Sadly, however, Amos' words went unheeded.

Like Amos, Hosea (called Osee in some older Bibles) prophesied in the northern kingdom from 750 to 725 B.C. Jeroboam II was the king of Israel at the beginning of Hosea's ministry. Anarchy and a quick succession of six kings followed Jeroboam's death. The Assyrian Empire repeatedly menaced Israel with threats, invasion and eventual conquest. Into this troubled situation the Lord sent his prophet Hosea to tell Israel—who had turned increasingly to the worship of pagan gods of neighboring nations—that their salvation lay not in armies and weapons but in a return to fidelity to the covenant. The words of the prophet Hosea describe his ordeal with his wife, Gomer, who increasingly preferred other men. The deterioration of the marriage of Hosea and Gomer parallels the deteriorating "marriage" of Yahweh and Israel. Gomer sells herself to other men; Israel sells herself to pagan gods. Generation after generation in Israel preferred to worship Baal and Asherah instead of Yahweh. The names of the three children born to Gomer bespeak the loss of love between those bound in the covenant of love: the children's names, in birth order, mean "God plants," "Not pitied," and "Not my people."

The words of Hosea are passionate, as one might expect from a man who deeply loves his wife, unfaithful though she is. Through the human words of the prophet, the Lord seems to go from anger to forgiveness several times. Longing to return to the years of his courtship of Israel, Yahweh summons his people to return to the wilderness: "I will allure her, and bring her into the wilderness, and speak tenderly to her" (2:14). The anguished intensity of the Lord's love for his unfaithful people finds its most eloquent expression in chapter 11.

Micah was a southerner, a contemporary of Isaiah of Jerusalem, but he came from the rural town of Moresheth. Micah prophesied in the latter part of the eighth century, as the Assyrian Empire was expanding its power. He criticized the wealthy, whose greed seemed boundless, and he warned against foolhardiness that thought Jerusalem unconquerable.

## Babylonian Dominance: The Last Years of Judah and during the Exile

All the prophets of this period addressed the southern kingdom, Judah.

Zephaniah preached during the earlier days of the reign of King Josiah, condemning sinful religious practices that Josiah eliminated in his reform of 622 B.C.

The prophet Nahum preached sometime before 612 B.C. (when Nineveh, the capital of the Assyrian Empire, was destroyed). Nahum gloated over the destruction of the city, which had come to symbolize for Judeans everything they hated about Assyrian domination.

We know virtually nothing about the prophet Habakkuk, other than the fact that he preached in the years immediately preceding the first deportation of exiles to Babylon in 597 B.C. Habakkuk boldly challenged God about his morality in letting the evil Babylonians inflict harm on Judah. God replied to the prophet that it must be that way for the present, for the Babylonians were instruments of judgment in his hands. But the Babylonians in their turn, as God assured his prophet, would be repaid for their own evil ways.

The Book of Obadiah is the shortest book in the Old Testament, just a single chapter. Its oracle against Edom is probably the preaching of this otherwise unknown prophet just after the destruction of Jerusalem in 587 B.C. Obadiah proclaimed God's condemnation of the Edomites who took advantage of Judah's misery. Verses 13 and 14 denounce Edom: "You should not have entered the gate of my people on the day of their calamity; you should not have joined in the gloating over Judah's disaster on the day of his calamity; you should not have looted his goods on the day of his calamity. You should not have stood at the crossings to cut off his fugitives; you should not have handed over his survivors on the day of distress." The antagonism between Judah and Edom was centuries old, and Obadiah was sure God would not fail to punish the Edomites for their actions against Judah at the time of the Babylonian conquest.

## Persian Dominance: The Period after the Exile

Cyrus, King of Persia, conquered the Babylonian Empire and allowed the Jewish exiles to return to Palestine. He also provided encouragement for the rebuilding of the Temple in Jerusalem. Although the work was begun shortly after the return from exile (538 B.C.), it soon faltered. In 520 B.C. the prophet Haggai delivered the five addresses included in the Book of Haggai, using his strong voice to call out a challenge to the leaders of the returned exiles to finish the work. Particularly telling is the challenging question to these leaders: "Is it a time for you yourselves to live in your paneled houses, while this house [the Temple] lies in ruins" (1:4)? Haggai was convinced that lasting prosperity could not return to Judah until the Lord's house, symbol of his abiding presence with his people, was properly rebuilt. The Temple was completed five years later.

Zechariah prophesied in Jerusalem from 520 to 518 B.C. and employed visions and dialogues with God to express his message. Like the Book of Isaiah, the Book of Zechariah contains words of the sixth-century prophet and also sizable additions by an unnamed prophet writing two or three centuries later. Chapters 1 through 8 are from sixth-century Zechariah; chapters 9 through 14 are the work of the prophet referred to as Second Zechariah.

The messages of these prophets have things in common, especially the conviction that Yahweh's renewed presence in the Temple would restore Jerusalem to greatness and that Yahweh would triumph over wickedness. The most famous verse in the preaching of the Second Zechariah is 9:9. The coming ruler of God's people is thus described: "Your king comes to you; triumphant and victorious is he, humble and riding on a donkey, on a colt, the foal of a donkey." Jesus enacted these words on Palm Sunday, thus appropriating to himself the title "Messiah."

We know nothing of the prophet Malachi, whose name merely means "my messenger." Likely preaching during the first half of the fifth century B.C., Malachi denounced abuses in the worship in the Second Temple, completed in 515 B.C. Lack of wholehearted devotion by the priests and the offering of blemished or sickly sacrificial animals are among Malachi's specific complaints.

The period of Joel's life and ministry is hard to ascertain. Some have dated his prophecy as early as the latter days of the kingdom of Judah. More likely, however, his preaching should be dated between 400 and 350 B.C. Joel was convinced that a "Day of Yahweh" was coming when Judah, if faithful to Yahweh, would be blessed and the nations hostile to Yahweh would be punished. Joel agreed with Haggai and Malachi in strongly supporting the Temple.

The Book of Jonah also is difficult to date, although a majority of scholars think it comes from the period after the Exile. It differs from the other eleven prophets in "the Twelve" because it is a story about a prophet rather than a record of that prophet's preaching. Pinning down the literary form of this book is a challenge. It is probably a short story that functions as an extended parable. Jonah tried to avoid going to preach to the hated Assyrians at their capital, Nineveh. And just as Jonah feared, the Assyrians repented and God did not inflict punishment on them. Jonah became very angry. He did not want God to be merciful to Nineveh; indeed he had longed to watch their punishment. So disappointed was Jonah in the repentance of Nineveh that he left the city and went out to pout. Instead of rejoicing at Nineveh's salvation, he was disappointed.

The details of this story do not coincide with history; in fact quite the opposite was true. There is no other record of God sending prophets to Israel's foes. And the city of Nineveh was, as we have seen, destroyed by the Babylonians in 612 B.C. So what is the point of the story? In the days after the Exile it was natural for the Jews to be resentful of many of their pagan neighbors. It was also natural for them to be preoccupied with their own needs. After all, they had lost much and had much rebuilding to do. To accomplish this rebuilding they had to reorganize themselves as a religious community. But the Book of Jonah warns against carrying the focus on themselves to an extreme. Jonah reminds the Jews that God was concerned not only with them but also with all of humankind.

# The Writings

## Wrestling with Tradition

The books of the Writings were produced within Judaism after the Babylonian Exile, and they are of a different character than the Torah and the Prophets. Nonetheless the authors of these books were steeped in the Torah and the Prophets, as their writings testify. In this rich collection we see post-exilic Judaism wrestling with the traditions of its faith and seeking to apply that faith to the circumstances of the time. We find in the Writings everything from hymns of praise to sensual poetry to basic good advice to short stories of persecution and perseverance. The amazing variety of voices in the Writings carried the powerful Word of God as he continued to speak to the Jewish people.

### On Faith, Praise and Hope

The Psalms were the hymnal God's people used in the days after the Exile. The Psalms (as we will see in the next chapter) express sorrow and joy, repentance and thanksgiving, pain and hope. The Song of Songs celebrates the depths of love, both human and divine, and the books of Ruth and Esther hold up models of faith for emulation. The history of God's people, especially the kingdom of Judah, is retold by the Chronicler (inspired author of 1 Chronicles and 2 Chronicles, Ezra and Nehemiah) in a different way than in the Deuteronomist's books of Samuel and Kings. The books of Chronicles are concerned that Yahweh be properly worshiped, for this was Israel's only hope for true renewal.

### On Suffering, Loss and Deliverance

The Book of Proverbs offers much advice, but it assumes that each person gets what he or she deserves: reward or punishment. The Book of Job on the other hand wrestles more deeply with human suffering, loudly asking "Why?" In his suffering, Job says: "I loathe my life; I will give free utterance to my complaint; I will speak in the bitterness of my soul. I will say to God, Do not condemn me; let me know why you contend against me. Does it seem good to you to oppress, to despise the work of your hands and favor the schemes of the wicked?" (10:1–3) Ultimately God responds: "Where were you when I laid the foundation of the earth? Tell me, if you have understanding. Who determined its measurements—surely you know! Or who stretched the line upon it? On what were its bases sunk, or who laid its cornerstone when the morning stars sang together and all the heavenly beings shouted for joy?" (38:4–7) The Book of Job leaves to God's providence the answer to why the just may suffer and the wicked may thrive.

The so-called "Five Scrolls" (Song of Songs, Ruth, Lamentations, Ecclesiastes and Esther) discuss love and loss and other serious questions about life. The scrolls are read at the annual festivals of the Jews: the Song of Songs at Passover (marking the Exodus from Egypt); Ruth at the Festival of Weeks or Pentecost (celebrating God's gift of the Sinai Covenant); Lamentations on the ninth day of the month of Av (mourning the destruction of the First and Second Temples, in 587 B.C. and 70 A.D., respectively); Ecclesiastes at the autumn feast of booths or tabernacles (commemorating Israel's forty years of living in booths in the wilderness); and Esther at the feast of Purim (celebrating the deliverance of the Jews during the Persian period).

## On Critical Post-Exilic Questions

The books of Ruth and Esther address the important post-exilic question about membership in God's people. For example, can foreigners become members? Can Judaism survive the continuing threats of hostile foreign powers? Using sensual imagery, the Song of Songs questions and probes human love—and for this reason, its inclusion among the Sacred Scriptures was problematic. Some found its frank language scandalous; others were puzzled because the book never mentions God. Jewish rabbis eventually accepted the Song of Songs as an allegory of the love between God and his bride, Israel. Christians apply the allegory to the love of Christ and his bride, the Church.

Ecclesiastes asks, What is the purpose of life under the sun? Ecclesiastes tells us that human wisdom can avail only so much. The ultimate purpose of life is understood by faith in God: "The end of the matter; all has been heard. Fear God, and keep his commandments; for that is the whole duty of everyone. For God will bring every deed into judgment, including every secret thing, whether good or evil (see 12:13–14). The best-known passage of the book (often through musical compositions) is the poem that begins in chapter 3, verse 1: "For everything there is a season, and a time for every matter under heaven."

Lamentations raises questions of fidelity ("Why have you forgotten us completely?" 5:20) and reminds us that the infidelity of God's people brought tragedy—the destruction of the Temple. Yet God restored the people after their period of repentance and conversion—the Exile.

Addressing questions of faith in the face of persecution, the Book of Daniel is included among the Prophets in Christian Bibles, but it is placed among the Writings in Jewish Bibles. Because the narrative unfolds during the Babylonian Exile, it was wrongly concluded in times past that the author belonged to the same period. Mainstream biblical scholars now agree that the book was written in the mid-second century B.C., during a time of crisis for the Jews paralleling that of the sixth century. The first half of the Book of Daniel contains stories about faithful Jews during the Babylonian Exile. The second half is written in the literary form known as *apocalypse*—which uses images and symbols to provide a message of hope and encouragement to people in the midst of a severe crisis (such as persecution). What appear to be predictions later fulfilled actually are historical facts the author already knows. The purpose of the book is to assure Jews enduring persecution at the hands of the Seleucid Greeks in the second century B.C. that Yahweh has not abandoned them and that perseverance in faith will once again save the nation.

## The Catholic Canon

The Catholic canon of the Old Testament also includes the books Tobit, Judith, Wisdom, Sirach, Baruch, and 1 Maccabees and 2 Maccabees. The Catholic canon also includes additions to the books of Esther and Daniel.

Sirach and Wisdom continue the wisdom tradition of Job, Proverbs and Ecclesiastes. Baruch the prophet was a disciple of Jeremiah. The short stories Tobit and Judith are meditations on God's providential care of individuals and of the whole Jewish people.

1 Maccabees and 2 Maccabees contain two independent accounts of the persecution of the Jews by the Greeks in the second century B.C. The books describe the actions of the Greek king Antiochus Epiphanes, who desecrated the Temple in 167 B.C. Antiochus put a statue of the pagan god Zeus into the innermost sanctuary, the Holy of Holies. He caused pigs (unclean for sacrifice to Yahweh) to be slaughtered on the Temple altar. Antiochus also made the practice of Judaism a capital offense. This precipitated the long but successful revolt of the Jews under the leadership of the Maccabee family. The rededication of the Temple to Yahweh is commemorated annually by the Jewish feast of Hanukkah.

# The Psalms

## Israel's Hymnbook
## and the Church's as Well

The Book of Psalms is actually a collection of five books, each ending in a short doxology or hymn of praise. Psalms 41, 72, 89 and 106 conclude the first four books, and there is a short doxology or hymn at the end of each. The conclusion of the fifth book and of the entire Psalter is a psalm of praise, Psalm 150.

Early collections of psalms seem to form the nuclei around which other psalms collected. In the first book (Psalms 1–41), several psalms are ascribed to King David. This is probably the basis of the notion that David is responsible for the whole collection, but this is clearly incorrect. Several psalms in the second and third books (Psalms 42–72 and Psalms 73–89) are attributed to Korah and Asaph, the guilds of temple singers in the Second Temple, built after the Exile. The fifth book (Psalms 107–150) contains psalms of praise known as the Hallel (or Hallelujah) Psalms.

The psalms traditionally fall into one of three categories: laments; psalms of praise, called hymns; and songs of thanksgiving. These are loose groupings, however, because some psalms reflect elements of more than one category, and a few psalms defy categorization altogether.

### Psalms of Lament

Nearly a third of the psalms are laments, a style that includes a plea for deliverance from misfortune, an expression of confidence in God, and a vow to perform an act of worship to thank God for intervening. Laments can be communal or individual. Examples of communal laments are Psalms 12, 14, 44, 90 and 137. Examples of individual laments are Psalms 3 through 7, 67 through 71, and 140 through 143. Psalm 7, an individual lament, illustrates the lament style:

O Lord my God, in you I take refuge;
    save me from all my pursuers, and deliver me,
or like a lion they will tear me apart;
    they will drag me away, with no one to rescue.
O Lord my God, if I have done this,
    if there is wrong in my hands,
if I have repaid my ally with harm
    or plundered my foe without cause,
then let the enemy pursue and overtake me,
    trample my life to the ground,
    and lay my soul in the dust.
Rise up, O Lord, in your anger;
    lift yourself up against the fury of my enemies;
    awake, O my God; you have appointed a judgment.
Let the assembly of the peoples be gathered around you,
    and over it take your seat on high.
The Lord judges the peoples;
    judge me, O Lord, according to my righteousness
    and according to the integrity that is in me.
O let the evil of the wicked come to an end,
    but establish the righteous,
you who test the minds and hearts,
    O righteous God.
God is my shield,
    who saves the upright in heart.
God is a righteous judge,
    and a God who has indignation every day.
If one does not repent, God will whet his sword;
    he has bent and strung his bow;
he has prepared his deadly weapons,
    making his arrows fiery shafts.
See how they conceive evil,
    and are pregnant with mischief,
    and bring forth lies.
They make a pit, digging it out,
    and fall into the hole that they have made.
Their mischief returns upon their own heads,

and on their own heads their violence descends.
I will give to the LORD the thanks due to his righteousness,
   and sing praise to the name of the Lord, the Most High.

The lament psalms sometimes cause problems for Christian morality, because some of them end with a curse upon enemies. For example, consider Psalm 137, a community lament over the destruction of Jerusalem, sometimes called the Song of the Exiles:

By the rivers of Babylon—
   there we sat down and there we wept
   when we remembered Zion.
On the willows there
   we hung up our harps.
For there our captors
   asked us for songs,
and our tormentors asked for mirth, saying,
   "Sing us one of the songs of Zion!"
How could we sing the Lord's song
   in a foreign land?
If I forget you, O Jerusalem,
   let my right hand wither!
Let my tongue cling to the roof of my mouth,
   if I do not remember you,
if I do not set Jerusalem
   above my highest joy.
Remember, O LORD, against the Edomites
   the day of Jerusalem's fall,
how they said, "Tear it down! Tear it down!
   Down to its foundations!"
O daughter Babylon, you devastator!
   Happy shall they be who pay you back
   what you have done to us!
Happy shall they be who take your little ones
   and dash them against the rock!

Today, of course, Christians simply cannot voice a prayer for the annihilation of a foreign nation by the brutal murder of its next generation. In Catholic liturgies the final verse of Psalm 137 (and similar curses in other psalms) is omitted.

## Psalms of Praise

Likely composed for liturgical use at festivals, the psalms often begin with a call to praise, perhaps by the leader of the liturgical assembly. Then God's wondrous deeds are recalled, and again God's praises are sung. Examples of hymns of praise include Psalms 8, 103, 104, 135 and 145 through 150. Psalm 146 illustrates the hymn:

Praise the LORD!
Praise the LORD, O my soul!
I will praise the Lord as long as I live;
   I will sing praises to my God all my life long.
Do not put your trust in princes,
   in mortals, in whom there is no help.
When their breath departs, they return to the earth;
   on that very day their plans perish.
Happy are those whose help is the God of Jacob,
   whose hope is in the LORD their God,
who made heaven and earth,
   the sea, and all that is in them;
who keeps faith forever;
   who executes justice for the oppressed;
   who gives food to the hungry.
The LORD sets the prisoners free;
   the LORD opens the eyes of the blind.
The LORD lifts up those who are bowed down;
   the LORD loves the righteous.
The LORD watches over the strangers;
   he upholds the orphan and the widow,
   but the way of the wicked he brings to ruin.
The LORD will reign forever,
   your God, O Zion, for all generations.
Praise the LORD!

## Songs of Thanksgiving and Others Psalms

Thanksgiving psalms are often difficult to categorize because many psalms contain a mixture of various themes. Psalms 9, 10 and 116 offer clear examples of songs of thanksgiving. Psalm 30 also is a song of thanksgiving, specifically for the recovery from a serious illness:

I will extol you, O LORD, for you have drawn me up,
  and did not let my foes rejoice over me.
O LORD my God, I cried to you for help,
  and you have healed me.
O LORD, you brought up my soul from Sheol,
  restored me to life from among those gone down to the Pit.
Sing praises to the LORD, O you his faithful ones,
  and give thanks to his holy name.
For his anger is but for a moment;
  his favor is for a lifetime.
Weeping may linger for the night,
  but joy comes with the morning.
As for me, I said in my prosperity,
  "I shall never be moved."
By your favor, O LORD,
  you had established me as a strong mountain;
you hid your face;
  I was dismayed.
To you, O LORD, I cried,
  and to the LORD I made supplication:
"What profit is there in my death,
  if I go down to the Pit?
Will the dust praise you?
  Will it tell of your faithfulness?
Hear, O LORD, and be gracious to me!
  O LORD, be my helper!"
You have turned my mourning into dancing;
  you have taken off my sackcloth
  and clothed me with joy,
so that my soul may praise you and not be silent.
  O LORD my God, I will give thanks to you forever.

Other kinds of psalms include those that were used on pilgrimages to the Temple— Psalms 120 through 134, for example. There are also psalms known as wisdom poems; examples include Psalms 1, 37, 112, 119 and 128.

One category of psalms was especially attractive to the early Church. Psalms 2, 18, 20, 21, 45, 72, 101, 110 and 144 are often called "messianic psalms." *Messiah* means "anointed," and these psalms refer in one way or another to the king, God's anointed. The early Church found new and deeper meaning in these psalms by reflecting on them in the light of its faith in Jesus. But the Messiah is not just a king; he is also one who suffered. As the Church reflected on Psalm 22, for example, it discovered another layer of understanding when it was applied to Jesus' suffering.

# The Canon

## How the Old Testament Came to Be

Critics of modern culture note that our age has little appreciation for history. We are so absorbed in the present and so concerned about what the future may hold that by comparison the past seems unimportant. Still, it is a truism that those who do not remember and learn from history are condemned to repeat it. Our present and our future are informed and fashioned by our past.

In the not too distant past, Christians in general made the mistake of overlooking the history underlying the Bible. This led to wrong assumptions about the meaning of the sacred texts, sometimes in contradiction to what God's Word actually means. By ignoring the human circumstances unique to each biblical book, biblical fundamentalists continue to repeat the mistake today.

In this overview, we have emphasized that the books of the Old Testament came into being within the concrete history of the nation of Israel in the two millennia before Christ. We have touched on the fact that each book has its own historical outlook and purpose and was composed by a human author or authors who were immersed in the concerns of Judaism at that particular moment in history. We have insisted that each book has a definite literary form that must be taken into account if its message is to be properly understood.

For all that, our real concern is not the history of Israel but the meaning of the Bible itself. Thus it would be a good idea to step back for a moment from the details of Old Testament history and ask how the Old Testament books came together as a whole.

We can distinguish three distinct stages in the formation of the Old Testament books: oral tradition, pre-biblical writing, and the final writing and editing of the texts as we know them today.

## Oral Tradition

The period of oral tradition extends from the time of the patriarchs, roughly the 1900s B.C. until records were first kept during the reigns of David and Solomon early in the tenth century B.C. Because we have few reliable written records, we know little about this period. We can reconstruct it as best we can only through a careful and respectful study and understanding of what comes afterward.

Remembrances about the patriarchs, Abraham, Isaac and Jacob, were kept alive by word of mouth from one generation to the next. But there was no one single tradition; there were "traditions." Each Hebrew tribe had a separate identity, and each settled in separate parts of Canaan—thus the stories of the patriarchs undoubtedly involved different versions and nuances for the different tribes.

The same thing is true for the Exodus itself, although here the events happened much closer to when they were recorded. Still, the historical facts of the Exodus were always filtered through a perspective of faith, with the primary concern being to reveal Yahweh's hand behind the events. Storytellers added colorful details to the bare facts. Thus it seems likely that each of the tribes developed its own way of narrating the Exodus.

## Pre-Biblical Writing

Exactly when the second period began, that of pre-biblical writing, we cannot be certain. We do know that the earliest Hebrew alphabet was borrowed from Canaan; and the Canaanites are credited with being the first to break free from pictorial writing, or using standard images to symbolize entire words. By developing an alphabet Canaan gave writing a precision and flexibility heretofore unknown. Even so, writing was a slow, laborious process for centuries and was an art few had the resources to master.

The earliest plausible time the Jews set any of their traditions in writing is during the era of the judges (1200–1025 B.C.), but it seems more likely that recording began later, probably during the reign of Solomon (970–931 B.C.). Only then had the Israelites established stability for themselves as a nation, and both the motives and the resources for preserving their traditions were clearly in place.

What was written down in the beginning also is a matter of speculation, for none of the earliest writings have survived. We do have some good clues, however. Given the importance for the nation, the oral traditions about the patriarchs and the Exodus surely must have been committed to writing. How these were shaped into a single narrative from the many oral sources is an interesting question, but we have no answer. We also know that after the division of Israel into two kingdoms (931 B.C.) each nation developed its own sacred writings and that the two written traditions were merged into one after 600 B.C. Again, we cannot be certain what principles guided the final editing process and what material was omitted from the combined version.

From the Book of Exodus (see 20:22–23:19; 24:7) we know of the existence of an earlier work called the "Book of the Covenant." The original Book of the Covenant may have been written as early as 950 B.C. and undoubtedly stated the legal implications of the Sinai Covenant for its day. The summary of this work contained in the Book of Exodus was written around 500 B.C. and was edited and updated in keeping with Judaic interests of that time. There also was a work identified as Deuteronomic written by priests in the 600s B.C. in connection with a reform movement. This work is the basis of our present Book of Deuteronomy and probably served as a norm for the editing of the entire Pentateuch.

## The Editing and Writing of the Biblical Books

The third stage, the editing and writing of the biblical books as we know them today, began during the Babylonian Exile in connection with the profound religious renewal Israel experienced at that time. How much writing was accomplished during the years of the Exile itself (587–538 B.C.) is unknown. The Book of Nehemiah (see 8:1–18) tells us that the Jews were overcome with emotion in 515 B.C. upon hearing the Book of the Law for the first time. This would indicate that only modest beginnings on the sacred writings occurred during the Exile and that many more years went by before even the Pentateuch was completed.

The editors of the sacred text had much raw material at hand: the sacred writings of both the northern and southern kingdoms, the Book of the Covenant, the Deuteronomic writings, and the works of the early prophets. To compose their introduction to the Pentateuch, the first eleven chapters of the Book of Genesis, they must have consulted ancient documents within Babylon itself.

The most critical factor in the editing process was deciding what to include, what to leave out, and how to make the finished product unified. The Deuteronomic material most likely provided the guidelines for making these decisions. The bottom-line conviction of the editors was that Yahweh had worked with Israel through its ups and downs for only one reason: to bring divine truth and salvation first to Israel and then to all nations. The Deuteronomic writers had indicated how this was to come about: by obedience to Yahweh's law.

## Divine Inspiration

The Jewish community rejected many of the circulated writings and accepted only those through which it believed God spoke. These the community "canonized" as divinely inspired books. *Canon* means "a final authoritative collection of books."

The process of canonization was lengthy, however. Individual books were composed, then joined into collections. First the Torah was compiled, followed by the collection of prophetic books—the Former and the Latter Prophets. The Writings were added last. We date the acceptance of these collections as authoritative Scripture (canonization) as follows: the Torah by 400 B.C., the Prophets by 200 B.C., and the Writings shortly before the time of Christ.

In the centuries after the Babylonian Exile, increasing numbers of Jews lived outside Palestine in Greek-speaking areas. These Jewish communities of the so-called Diaspora (Dispersion) revered additional books not included in the canon recognized by the Jews in Palestine. These additional books and parts of other books are known as deuterocanonical (that is, belonging to the "second" canon). Roman Catholic and Orthodox Christians accept this larger canon; many Protestants and most Jews do not. The Septuagint translation of the Hebrew Bible into Greek, produced by Greek-speaking Jews in ancient Egypt, included the deuterocanonical books accepted by the Diaspora Jews.

## Development in Doctrine

It is worth noting that the books of the Old Testament show development in doctrine. The earlier Scriptures, for example, reflect a tolerance of understandings and practices that later Scriptures reject. We also see how the acceptance of many gods during patriarchal times gradually gives way to uncompromising monotheism. Polygamy, viewed in a favorable light in the stories of the patriarchs, is eventually rejected as contrary to God. Inhuman treatment of captives of war, accepted in Deuteronomy as a practical necessity, is opposed in later writings. Serious doubt about the fundamental question of life after death gives way in the end to clear and explicit belief.

This simple review of doctrinal development demonstrates how misguided we are to assume we can read any given verse of sacred Scripture as God's final revelation on the subject. God never frees us of the responsibility to handle Sacred Scripture for what it is: the gradual unfolding of divine truth through the limitations of human authors. As the accumulated wisdom of Judaism increased over time, the fuller dimensions of God's Word increasingly came into view.

# The Anointed One

## Was the Coming of Christ Foretold?

Have you ever wondered why most of Jesus' fellow Jews did not recognize him as the Messiah? Not long ago Catholics assumed God had planted clear predictions about Jesus throughout the Old Testament books, predictions that an impartial reader should easily recognize. Thus it always seemed puzzling that the Jews of Jesus' day did not pick up on these and more readily accept him as the Messiah.

More fundamentalist Christians still treat many Old Testament prophecies as predictions about Jesus. Research by Catholic scholars (joined by that of many Protestant and Orthodox scholars), however, has given us a better understanding of Old Testament prophecy. We find that many of the Old Testament texts that have been applied to Jesus are anything but crystal-clear in this regard in their original context. It is only as a result of our faith in Jesus that we are able to see deeper meanings in many Old Testament passages.

### The Birth of Messianic Hope

Old Testament texts that refer to a future savior are called "messianic prophecies." *Messiah* is a Hebrew word meaning "the anointed one." The future savior was to be a blood descendant of King David. Because kings are anointed in the enthronement ceremony, the future savior came to be referred to as "the anointed one."

The Greek word for messiah is "Christ." Jesus was publicly proclaimed to be the "Christ" or the "Messiah" only after his resurrection. Before that he was known simply as Jesus of Nazareth. When we use the term *Jesus Christ*, we are not so much naming Jesus as we are professing our faith that he is the Messiah.

The foundational text for messianic thinking is 2 Samuel 7.

Sometime during the reign of King David (ca. 1000-970 B.C.) the prophet Nathan told David that he and his descendants were to be the "house" of God's covenant with Israel. This meant that for all generations the royal lineage of David was to provide enduring security for Yahweh's covenant relationship with the Israelites.

Centuries later, when Jerusalem collapsed before the Babylonian invaders, the Davidic line of kings came to an abrupt end. During their exile in Babylon, however, the Jews learned to hope once again for a future—and from that time forward the text from 2 Samuel 7 held new meaning.

As the exiled Jews saw it, God would restore their lost kingdom under the leadership of a descendant of David—if they would simply renew their devotion to the Sinai Covenant. Thus messianic hope was born. The sacred writings were reread to look for other indications of messianic prophecy, and indeed many were found. For example, Amos 9:11–15 was taken to refer to the age of the coming Messiah.

The exiles who returned to Palestine in 538 B.C. were buoyed up by the thoughts of Israel's coming independence under a restored Davidic kingship. Fidelity to the Sinai Covenant, as detailed in the Book of the Law (the Pentateuch), was understood to be the infallible means by which Israel's dream would be realized. As Persian domination dragged on, however, disillusion set in and people began to ask what was wrong: Why was Yahweh so slow to fulfill his covenant promise?

## Keeping Hope Alive

It was in this atmosphere that the last Old Testament writers made their appearance. We can distinguish three phases in the unfolding of their messages.

During the first phase, the prophets Haggai and Zechariah, both of whom wrote in 520 B.C., concentrated on the need to complete the rebuilding of the Temple in Jerusalem. Haggai said that Yahweh was displeased with the Israelites because of their failure to complete the Temple, implying that all would be well when the Temple was finally finished. Zechariah had much the same message, although he went further, saying that messianic hopes would be fulfilled as soon as Israel's conduct as a nation conformed perfectly to Yahweh's law. Zechariah possibly hints in an obscure text that there would be two messiahs (see 4:14) who would rule in perfect harmony (see 6:13): one a head of state and the other a high priest.

During the second phase, the prophets Malachi and Joel placed the theme of the "day of Yahweh" at the center of messianic expectation. Writing in the 400s or early 300s B.C., Malachi and Joel confronted a people increasingly despondent—and small wonder. The Temple had been finished and sacrifices were once more being performed as the highest ritual expression of Judaic law, yet the nation's fortunes were showing no improvement. Rather the dream of a triumphant Israel, supreme among nations as the chosen people of Yahweh, seemed to recede further and further. Borrowing from a theme of Ezekiel, the prophet of the Babylonian Exile, Malachi and Joel linked the future messianic age with a total transformation of world history. The coming "day of Yahweh" would bring judgment upon humankind as a whole: The good, including all faithful Israelites, would be ushered into everlasting happiness, and the evil would be sentenced to lasting punishment.

In the third phase, we find the Book of Daniel, written in approximately 166 B.C., just before the Maccabean Wars (164–143 B.C.), speaking the final word on messianism prior to Jesus' birth. The Book of Daniel as a whole offers hope and reassurance to a people under severe religious persecution at the hand of the Greeks. The author of the Book of Daniel sets his narrative in the years of the Babylonian Exile. Daniel, the hero of the story, not only survives persecution but is championed by Yahweh. The meaning is clear: If the Jews hold fast to Yahweh in the present persecution, they too will overcome.

The author of the Book of Daniel also looks to the future, repeating in highly symbolic images the message of his predecessors Malachi and Joel. This curious form of biblical expression is called *apocalypse*, and it shows up again in the final book of the New Testament, the Book of Revelation.

The author of Daniel describes the coming messiah as "one like a son of man coming on the clouds of heaven" (7:13), whose sovereign domain over all nations of the earth will last forever (see 7:14). Originally the "son of man" probably referred to the Jewish people as a whole. Matthew, Mark and Luke later apply this passage to Jesus in order to emphasize that *he* is the Messiah Israel had been awaiting for so long.

## Understanding by Looking Backward

Old Testament messianic writings as a whole, including certain psalms, contain numerous texts that we Christians rightly apply to Jesus. We must not forget, however, that we make these applications by looking "backward," so to speak—by first believing that Jesus is the Savior of the world and that he is, therefore, the Messiah of Israel. The situation for Jesus' contemporaries, however, was far different.

At the time Jesus began his public career there was nothing approaching a uniform understanding of the messianic prophecies. Some held that there wouldn't even be a personal messiah, regarding the "day of Yahweh" as so definitive that it could not possibly be mediated by a human being. Even those who did believe in the coming of a personal messiah had conflicting, even contradictory, notions about him.

The central expectation was that the messiah was to be a "son of David," one who would win Israel's independence and assume kingship. By all appearances Jesus didn't qualify. The one time Jesus' contemporaries tried to force kingship on him, he would have none of it (see John 6:15).

A second common expectation was that the messiah would be a priest; we have alluded to this viewpoint as it was displayed in Zechariah (see 4:14; 6:13). Because the priestly class had functioned as leaders in the place of kings since 587 B.C., messianism quite naturally gave increasing prominence to priests. Yet Jesus was neither a temple priest nor a member of a priestly class. He was a layman.

There were two less widely held notions about the future messiah. One was that he would be a prophet; the other that he would be a "wise man" in the best tradition of the Wisdom writings. As it worked out, these were the very images that best applied to Jesus in the course of his lifetime. Only after the resurrection did the first Christians discover in the risen Jesus both kingship and priesthood in a sense far surpassing anything his contemporaries could possibly have known.

# Part II
# The New Testament

# Overview

## The Kingdom of God

The books of the New Testament were written against the background of the first century, a time of massive change for the Jewish nation. In 70 A.D. the Romans destroyed Jerusalem and its Temple, leaving the Jewish people without an official sacrificial system, since the Temple had been their central sanctuary. The year 70 A.D. also is an important reference point for the development of New Testament writings and of Christianity as a whole. Before that time Judaism still was regarded as an integral part of Christianity, in spite of the fact that the apostle Paul had spearheaded an important change in this way of thinking prior to his death. Until 70 A.D., the chief centers of Christianity—Jerusalem, Antioch and Rome—held the essentials of Judaism to be integral to Christian faith and practice. After 70 A.D., however, the situation began to change rapidly. More and more, Christianity emerged as a religion complete in itself and separate from Judaism.

None of the books of the New Testament existed during the first two decades of Christianity, from 30 to 50 A.D. The Church, however, was alive in the power of the Holy Spirit and in the preaching of the gospel by word of mouth. This was the time of oral tradition, similar to the periods of oral tradition in Old Testament times, though much shorter. Until just before the end of this twenty-year period, virtually all Christians were Jews and most of them lived in or near Jerusalem. Certainly the apostles preached throughout Palestine and journeyed to some major Jewish settlements in the Diaspora, but for the most part they remained headquartered in Jerusalem until after 50 A.D.

### An Infant Church

Christianity in its infancy was thoroughly "Jewish." The foundational teaching about Jesus was that he was Israel's long-awaited Messiah. Having been raised from the dead and enthroned in heaven by Yahweh, Jesus was now preparing Israel for the "day of Yahweh," which would follow soon. All who accepted Jesus as the Messiah were to prepare for his final coming by turning from sin and being baptized.

Christianity maintained that the deepest religious longings of the Jewish people were at last being realized in and through Jesus. Not only was this message completely compatible with Judaism, but commitment to Judaism seemed to be required if the message were to be understood and accepted. It is little wonder, then, that the apostles continued to congregate around Jerusalem, remaining faithful at first to the Judaism of their heritage.

The first books of the New Testament were written in the second twenty years of Christianity, from 50 to 70 A.D. Except for the Gospel of Mark all these early works were letters written by church leaders in response to specific problems or concerns. Examples are the letters of Paul and possibly 1 Peter. Mark wrote his Gospel, understood to be the oldest of the Gospels, around 70 A.D., probably just after Peter's martyrdom in Rome (ca. 64-67 A.D.)—and no doubt there is a connection between these two events. As the apostles began to disappear from the scene of history, there was a need for a written summary of the beliefs they proclaimed about Jesus. Although Mark's Gospel is the earliest such document to come down to us, others shortly followed.

Between 50 and 70 A.D., Christians began to conclude that the "day of Yahweh," or the final coming of Jesus, appeared to be further off than had been originally assumed. Mark states quite pointedly: "But about that day or hour no one knows, neither the angels in heaven, nor the Son, but only the Father" (13:32).

Once this awareness sank in, organizational aspects of Christianity suddenly took on greater importance. For example, things such as the leadership and interrelationship of the various Christian communities, liturgical practices, and the formulation of Christian beliefs all needed much more concentrated attention. The Church became concerned about the structures that held it together and upon which its future survival depended. In this context Peter's role as leader of the apostles grew increasingly significant.

## An Expanding Faith

Also between 50 and 70 A.D., what Christianity meant for Gentiles (non-Jews) was explored, debated and increasingly clarified. The apostle Paul energized these developments by making three extensive missionary journeys before his death in Rome in about 67 A.D. During his first journeys, 46-51 A.D., Paul found among Gentiles a willing audience for his preaching concerning Jesus, at times even more so than among Jews. Once he decided to baptize Gentiles, Paul had to make a crucial decision: Should he require them to accept Judaism as well? He concluded that accepting Judaism was not necessary to becoming a Christian and proceeded to set up Christian communities made up almost entirely of non-Jews.

When Paul returned to Jerusalem in 51 A.D., however, he had to answer to the other apostles for what he had done. This was the setting for the so-called Council of Jerusalem described in the Acts of the Apostles 15:6–29. At this gathering of the leaders of the young Church, Paul argued that the time from Abraham until Jesus had been a preparation for the coming of the Messiah, whose reign was to extend eventually to all nations. If Jesus was the Christ, he said, then the period of preparation was now over and Gentiles as well as Jews should therefore be welcomed into Christianity. Furthermore, if salvation comes simply from faith that Jesus is the Christ, then the religion of Judaism is not necessary for salvation and Gentiles need not observe its laws. Paul's argument carried the day, and he became known as "the Apostle of the Gentiles."

Because the other apostles continued to seek Jews as the primary target for conversion, however, tension between the two forms of Christian communities inevitably developed. Some Jewish believers continued to claim that they were the only ones who were "fully" Christian and that Gentile believers were something less. In addition, even among Jewish Christians there were significant differences of opinion regarding true doctrine and practice. It was during this time of tension that the later books of the New Testament were written, including the Gospels of Matthew and Luke (ca. 85 A.D.) and John (ca. 95 A.D.).

## The Case for Christianity

The gospel writers combine two time frames: the time of Jesus' past (his birth, life, death and resurrection) and his present situation (risen, alive and actively at work in the midst of the community of believers). The Evangelists use Jesus' past as a foundation on which to build a portrait of Jesus as the reigning Messiah. Because the two time frames are so perfectly wedded it is sometimes all but impossible to distinguish between them. Attempting to read the Gospels solely as history is something like listening to a symphony while trying to ignore the sounds of half the orchestra. The reverse is also true, however. The gospel narratives cannot be read as fiction. Because the Evangelists were well aware that the case for Christianity stands or falls on the basis of Jesus' personal history, they took pains to speak accurately about the person of Jesus, his death, and his resurrection. The problem, if we may call it that, again concerns how the Evangelists present the facts. They do not assume the pose of dispassionate historians. They speak as passionate believers, eager to bring out the meaning of past events in the light of Jesus' present messianic reign.

The basic literary form of the Gospels, then, is faith-proclamation, not scientific history. The Evangelists narrate Jesus' earthly history not to preserve the bare facts but to bring their readers to believe in Jesus. They add insights born of post-resurrection faith to the events they record: "These are written so that you may come to believe that Jesus is the Messiah, the Son of God, and that through believing you may have life in his name" (John 20:31).

Thus when we hear the phrase "at that time" Jesus said or did such and such, we are not necessarily dealing with chronological history. We are most likely dealing with the Evangelist's professed faith in the fuller meaning behind Jesus' original words and actions, a meaning that came to light only after the resurrection. We cannot, therefore, lift individual texts from the Gospels and draw conclusions about what Jesus himself said or did. Rather, we honor the Gospels as proclamations that Jesus is the Christ—proclamations made by men whose vision blends their present belief with past events.

At the same time we need have no doubt concerning the factual accuracy of the overall portrait of Jesus given by the Gospels. As we shall see, each Evangelist had his own purpose in writing and his own readership in mind. Yet the same unmistakable and consistent image of Jesus shines through each Gospel. The portrait of Jesus is so uniquely attractive, at once so holy and so forthright in action, that it could have been inspired only by the same real human being.

## The Kingdom of God

All the Evangelists are one in saying that Jesus' basic message was that the messianic kingdom, "the kingdom of God," was at hand. They all state that Jesus proclaimed this message tirelessly, explaining it through many parables. Jesus said that love is the dynamic by which God's kingdom comes into being. As God himself relates in love to humans, so God enjoins all to love one another without discrimination. To prove the point, Jesus devoted much of his ministry to those who were discriminated against: the poor, the diseased, the sinners and even the hated Samaritans and other foreigners.

In all four Gospels, the heart of the message is found in the accounts of Jesus' death and resurrection. Upon analysis, the goodness of Jesus in his lifetime, however singular, is of no account except for what followed: "If Christ has not been raised, then our proclamation has been in vain and your faith has been in vain" (1 Corinthians 15:14).

It is no wonder, then, that the death-resurrection narratives take up such a large portion of each Gospel. The Evangelists want to underscore that Jesus truly died and, even more importantly, that he was truly raised to new life by the direct intervention of God. On these two events the credibility of the Gospels depends. Because he has died and is risen, Jesus of Nazareth has become the Messiah, the Savior of the world.

Even in the death-resurrection narratives we find the Evangelists' faith at the forefront. They do not suddenly become literal historians once they reach the climax of their work. Rather they remain commentators in faith as to the meaning of Jesus' dying and rising. Thus, for example, the four resurrection accounts have discrepancies in detail about who, where, and in what sequence people encountered the risen Lord. Clearly the Evangelists were not concerned about such details. Their all-absorbing concern was to plant the taproot of Christian faith: Jesus, having died, is forever alive in a very real way and reigns in power over the kingdom of God. Each writer does this in his own way, always calling for faith, repentance from sin, and baptism. These themes are repeatedly emphasized in each of the Gospels.

## The New Testament Canon

Unfortunately this short survey cannot give a book-by-book description of how the New Testament canon was formed. The communities to whom Paul wrote probably sent copies of his letters to neighboring Christian communities. Many Pauline churches would therefore have had a small collection of the apostle's letters. The writing of the Acts of the Apostles, with its large amount of material about Paul, may have spurred increased interest in his letters. It's possible that at this time (around 85 A.D.) certain smaller collections were grouped to form larger ones. All we can say is that by around 100 A.D., the letters of Paul were considered to be Sacred Scripture—on a par with the Torah, the Prophets and the Writings of the Old Testament. "So also our beloved brother Paul wrote to you according to the wisdom given him, speaking of this as he does in all his letters. There are some things in them hard to understand, which the ignorant and unstable twist to their own destruction, as they do the other *scriptures*" (2 Peter 3:15-16, emphasis added).

The Gospels, circulated independently, eventually were collected as well. By a long process of reflection by the Church, the four we now have were added to the canon, while other writings in the style of a gospel were rejected. It would be several centuries (around 400 A.D.) before the Church at large agreed on the twenty-seven works that now make up the New Testament. Christians believe, however, that the Holy Spirit guided the entire process, to the point that we say these—and only these—New Testament documents were divinely inspired in the same way as those of the Old Testament.

# Mark and Matthew

## "The Beginning of the Good News"

**M**ark, considered the oldest of the four Gospels, begins his account with "The beginning of the good news of Jesus Christ, the Son of God." Thus it is interesting to note that Luke opens his Gospel by speaking of other authors who wrote about Jesus: "Many have undertaken to set down an orderly account of the events that have been fulfilled among us" (1:1). We know that when Luke penned these words, around 85 A.D., Mark was in fact the only one of the four New Testament Evangelists who had already written. Clearly, then, Luke was referring to other "gospels" besides Mark's. Scholars now tell us that more than twenty gospel-style manuscripts were written in the first century, with names such as "The Gospel of Thomas," "The Gospel of Mary," "The Gospel of James," and even "The Gospel of Judas."

### Why These Four?

If there were so many first-century gospels recounting the life and times of Jesus Christ, why are the four Gospels known to us today— Matthew, Mark, Luke and John—in the New Testament while others are not? Although we do not have a full answer to this question, it is enough for us to admit that the Holy Spirit deserves all credit in this matter. Yet humanly speaking we do know that the process by which the four Gospels in the New Testament came to be singled out as God's Word was lengthy and at times seemingly haphazard.

No one predetermined how many Gospels there should be. Nor was it immediately evident to the Church, when our present Gospels had been completed, that these particular works were superior to many other similar writings. The Church first had to live with all such works for many years, savoring what each had to offer. Only after a long sifting process did the Gospels of Matthew, Mark, Luke and John alone survive.

We might also ask why we need four Gospels. Would not one suffice? One commentator has whimsically suggested that we imagine the four Evangelists on an editorial board that has been commissioned to choose the one Gospel that would be the standard Church proclamation. Mark might suggest that his presentation is the best because he emphasizes the humanity of Jesus and the need for Christians to embrace the suffering of Jesus. Matthew, however, might insist that his account better represents Christianity as flowering forth from the stalk of Judaism. Luke might lobby for his writing because of his optimistic tone and his emphasis on Jesus as the Lord of history. Finally John, whose Gospel is quite different from the other three, might bemusedly laugh at the other Evangelists and say that his should be the standard proclamation of the Church because he presents Jesus as the divine Son of God made man, thus clearly making his account the superior Gospel. In fact all four were retained precisely because no one of them tells the entire story of Jesus. Each sheds light in a uniquely important way on the original message as preached by the apostles.

The four Evangelists all proclaimed the good news of Jesus of Nazareth, who was a real human being and walked the earth at a specific time. It would seem, then, that we could expect a measure of uniformity in their four works. They do agree on the basics of the story, yet each account is unique.

## Why the Differences?

The differences found among the four Gospels were explained in the 1964 document from the Pontifical Biblical Commission *Instruction Concerning the Historical Truth of the Gospels*. This document recognizes three stages in the development of the gospel message: the historical life of Jesus; the preaching of the early Church concerning the meaning of Jesus' life, death and resurrection; and finally the written Gospels. The Gospels are based much more on the second stage, the years of oral tradition and preaching about Jesus, than on historical facts about his life. What is important to remember is that the four documents we call *Gospels* are applications of the message of the Risen Christ by inspired authors who were addressing particular needs of their faith communities.

We should note in passing that the actual authors of the Gospels are technically unknown. The designations "according to" are not part of the inspired text. The attributions to specific people in the apostolic tradition were added later to signify that the early Church accepted these works as faithful to that tradition.

Scholars group together the Gospels of Mark, Matthew and Luke under the name *synoptic*. In Greek the word *synoptic* literally means "look alike." Even a casual comparison of these three Gospels shows that they do, in fact, appear to be similar. John's Gospel, on the other hand, stands apart as distinctly different.

## Mark: What Being a Christian Really Means

We know that Mark's was the first Gospel written and that Matthew and Luke made extensive use of Mark's Gospel in writing their own. This explains why the three Gospels appear to be so similar. Mark's highly inventive and forceful way of narrating the Jesus event served as a model for Luke and Matthew.

We know next to nothing about Mark himself. We do know, however, that he was not an apostle. An early tradition suggested that he was a traveling companion of Peter, possibly serving as Peter's scribe or interpreter on missionary journeys. We also know that Mark's Gospel was written around 70 A.D., just before or at the same time that Rome was destroying Jerusalem. For several reasons this was a time of tremendous crisis for the infant Church.

A Jewish sect known as the Zealots had seized control of Jerusalem and was frantically proclaiming that the "day of Yahweh" was at last at hand. Rome responded to this uprising by laying siege to the city, building toward the final onslaught two years later. Centered in Jerusalem, the Christian Church thus found itself doubly under fire—from the Zealots inside the city and from the Romans outside. To make matters worse, Peter and Paul, the two central figures of the Church from its beginning, had been put to death in Rome. And after a series of national calamities the emperor Nero was using Christians as scapegoats, executing them with sadistic cruelty. As a result many Christians were defecting, concluding that the claims of Jesus had been unmasked as false thanks to the harsh realities confronting the Church.

Such is the background against which Mark writes. A subtitle for Mark's Gospel might be "What Being a Christian Really Means." Mark vigorously attacks any notion that Christian discipleship means security in this life. Yes, Jesus is risen, he says; and yes, Jesus is the reigning Messiah preparing the world for the final coming of the kingdom of God. But in this in-between time the experience of Jesus' followers can be no different than that of Jesus himself. For what the Risen Lord says to the presently troubled Christian community is this: "If any want to become my followers, let them deny themselves and take up their cross and follow me. For those who want to save their life will lose it, and those who lose their life for my sake, and for the sake of the gospel, will save it" (8:34–35).

Mark's entire composition develops this one theme. Three successive segments of his Gospel follow the same pattern. Each climaxes in a prediction of the crucifixion (Mark 8:31; 9:31; 10:33) and a call to follow Jesus by embracing the sufferings that God inevitably requires of Christians. In each case the apostles, the first disciples of Jesus, are presented as befuddled and uncomprehending—as if to say that grasping the basic meaning of discipleship never comes easily.

Although Mark's Gospel is similar to that of Matthew and Luke it does have its own character. A feature unique to Mark's Gospel, for example, is the vividness with which Jesus' humanness comes through. Mark does not hesitate to say that Jesus could be passionately angry (see 3:5), that he could be ignorant at times (see 5:30; 13:32), and that he did not always achieve what he wanted (see 6:5). Mark alone tells us that Jesus' blood relatives considered him "out of his mind" (3:21). Mark gives as Jesus' dying words a cry filled with human anguish: "My God, my God, why have you deserted me?" (15:34). Matthew, Luke and John are much more cautious about the "weaknesses" of Jesus and deliberately downplay these Markan passages.

## Matthew: A Christian Torah

The best evidence suggests that the Gospels of Matthew and Luke both were written around the year 85 A.D., each author probably unaware of what the other was doing. Both Gospels clearly borrow heavily from Mark but not directly from each other. At the same time both authors undoubtedly made use of other sources. Like Mark, neither author was himself an apostle, and neither presented his material as that of an eyewitness. Both wrote a summary of the Church's contemporary understanding of and preaching about Jesus.

By 85 A.D. things had started to settle down a bit for the Church. The crisis of Jerusalem's destruction was past, and Christianity had survived. Nero had ended his own life, and for the time being Roman persecution of Christians had abated. Gentile Christians loomed as the wave of the future, and the formerly strong link to Jerusalem was beginning to dissolve. No longer able to have Jerusalem as it geographic center, the Church increasingly developed a universal outlook. Where Christians lived in large numbers, as in Antioch, Alexandria and Rome, new leadership for the Church began to emerge.

Matthew's Gospel was written primarily for Jewish Christians. This is evident in the author's many allusions to the Old Testament and his references to customs and situations that only Jews would readily understand. The primary theme of the Gospel is that Judaism has not been cast aside by Christianity; rather Christianity flowers forth from the stalk of Judaism: "Do not think that I have come to abolish the law or the prophets; I have come not to abolish but to fulfill" (5:17). Matthew, in fact, presents Jesus as a new Moses, and Jesus—like Moses—teaches at length. Some suggest that Matthew set out to present a "Christian Torah."

Matthew wrote about a decade and a half after the Romans destroyed Jerusalem. When temple worship was no longer possible, a new form of Judaism began to emerge as rabbis adapted Judaism in response to the new circumstances. At the same time the early Christians were proclaiming faith in Jesus as the new route for Judaism. The conflict between rabbinic Judaism and the Jewish Christian community of Matthew is clear from the pages of this Gospel.

Matthew includes stories of Jesus' birth and infancy, obviously intending these to be symbolic. The gifts of the magi, for example, announce Matthew's understanding that Jesus is Israel's Messiah. Gold proclaims his kingship; frankincense recognizes his divinity; myrrh (used in embalming) announces that Jesus is the Suffering Servant of the Lord. Jesus will fulfill his role as Messiah in his sufferings on the cross.

Despite the Jewishness of Matthew's Gospel, however, it ends on a note that recognizes that the future of the Church is with the Gentiles. The Risen Christ tells his disciples: "All authority in heaven and on earth has been given to me. Go therefore and make disciples of all nations, baptizing them in the name of the Father and of the Son and of the Holy Spirit, and teaching them to obey everything that I have commanded you. And remember, I am with you always, to the end of the age" (28:18–20). Jesus' promise to be with his Church always fulfills his designation as Emmanuel, God-with-us (see 1:23).

# Luke and Acts

## "An Orderly Account of the Events"

Of the four Gospels, Luke's alone required a follow-up in order to get its central theme across. Mark's image of Jesus, of a Messiah who brings about God's reign through suffering, is complete at the close of his Gospel. Matthew and John also complete their pictures of Jesus in their Gospels. Matthew sees Jesus as the fulfillment of God's revelation in the Old Testament; John presents Jesus as the divine Son of God made man. Luke's approach, however, is to understand Jesus as Lord of history. To make this notion clear Luke had to follow his Gospel with the Acts of the Apostles.

Luke was highly aware of the new situation in which the Christian Church found itself after the destruction of Jerusalem in 70 A.D. Up to this time the Church had been strongly wedded to Judaism, with many believers still regarding Christianity as a branch of Judaism. In the wake of Judea's collapse, however, these Jewish-oriented Christians tended toward despair. In addition, the Church's future seemed even more bleak in the absence of Peter, Paul and—probably by that time—most of the other apostles.

### Luke: Jesus in the Spotlight

Amid this gloom Luke is an uncompromising optimist, reviewing the Church's current crisis not as the end of Christianity but as its true beginning. As Luke sees it, Jesus is not so much the Messiah of Israel as he is the Lord of history, the Savior of the entire world. In order to share this vision with others, Luke sets it to writing.

Luke divides history into three stages: the time before Jesus, the time during Jesus' lifetime, and the time after Jesus' death and resurrection. The first two stages are handled in his Gospel, and the third is told in the Acts of the Apostles. This threefold division of history is not limited to the Church, however. It embraces all of creation, secular history as well as Christianity, from beginning to end. Like Paul, Luke regards Jesus Christ as the keystone upon which the entire cosmos depends for its meaning and fulfillment.

The first stage of history, "before Jesus," came to a close with John the Baptist: "The law and the prophets were in effect until John came" (Luke 16:16). This is to say that all previous history, climaxing with John the Baptist, was a preparation for the appearance of Jesus.

To make his point even clearer Luke takes liberties with Mark's account of Jesus' baptism by John. Luke wants to have the stage cleared of John, so to speak, once Jesus is on the scene. So Luke reports that right at the beginning of Jesus' public life John is arrested by Herod and shut up in prison (see 3:19–20). He doesn't even mention John's presence at Jesus' baptism (see 3:21). According to Luke, the spotlight of history must be upon Jesus alone.

The second stage of history, "Jesus himself," is taken up with Jesus' actions in readying the world for its third and climactic stage: the birth of the Church. To strengthen this particular understanding of Jesus' career, Luke uses a geographical device. Because Jerusalem is the central place, Luke anticipates its importance for his Gospel by having Jesus go there with much eagerness as a child (see 2:41–50).

It was in Jerusalem that Jesus' work attained completion and where the third and final stage of history began with the Pentecost event. Thus beginning with chapter 9, verse 51, Luke portrays Jesus as constantly journeying toward Jerusalem. Jesus does not get there until ten chapters later (see 19:41). But in the interim we are repeatedly reminded that Jesus is relentlessly on the way, determined to get there (see 13:22; 17:11; 19:11).

Meanwhile the themes unfolding in Luke's narrative have a distinctive flavor when compared to the other Gospels. In particular, Luke's account of Jesus' infancy is strikingly different from Matthew's. For both Evangelists these childhood accounts form a creative introduction to their main gospel themes. As their themes were quite different, so their infancy narratives are equally different.

In Luke's Gospel, as one commentator put it, Jesus seems to be always going to, sitting at, or coming from a meal. Luke uses these meals to teach about forgiveness and love, thus forming an important theme within the Gospel as a whole.

Other Gospels give more play to the political and religious intrigue that eventually resulted in Jesus' execution. Although Luke does not overlook this, he prefers to stress the universalist aspect of Jesus' work. To make this concrete Luke concentrates on people who in his time were considered social misfits: the poor, sinners, women, and non-Jews. Luke has Jesus consistently going out of his way to favor such persons. Thus Luke tells his contemporaries that all people are invited into full standing as beneficiaries of Jesus' messianic reign. In other words, the future of the Church is not limited to the Jewish people or to Jewish social views.

The second stage of history, wholly taken up with the physical presence of Jesus on earth, came to a close with his bodily departure. For Luke this occurs not with Jesus' death but with the end of Jesus' resurrection appearances. Significantly, Luke designates the time of Jesus' appearances after the resurrection as "forty days," a biblical number signifying a period of intense preparation. Thus with the account of Jesus' Ascension Luke brings his gospel narrative to a close midstream—and leaves his readers eager for what is yet to come: "He withdrew from them and was carried up into heaven" (24:51).

## Acts: The Narrative Continues

The Acts of the Apostles takes up Luke's narrative exactly where his Gospel leaves off. The story of the Ascension is repeated, and a sense of keen expectation is built as the apostles are told: "You will receive power when the Holy Spirit has come upon you" (1:8a). Luke at once revives his geographical device, although this time it works in reverse. Instead of having Jerusalem serve as the end point, it is now the starting point: "You will be my witnesses in Jerusalem, in all Judea and Samaria, and to the ends of the earth" (1:8b).

This clues us in on what will follow. Like ripples from the center of a pond, the saving work of Jesus is to extend ever outward in larger circles, eventually embracing all humankind. Luke first recounts the birth of the Church in Jerusalem (see chapters 1–5). He then offers a series of accounts of missionary journeys, climaxing with Paul's "proclaiming the kingdom of God and teaching about the Lord Jesus Christ with all boldness and without hindrance" (28:31) in Rome, the center of the entire world as Luke knew it.

Given that Paul had been dead for about twenty years when Luke wrote Acts, we have to ask why Acts ends as it does, with Paul enjoying great success in preaching the gospel at Rome. Why didn't Luke go on to tell of Paul's final imprisonment and martyrdom? Luke is very intentional in this regard: his primary concern is not to recount historical facts but to convey his vision of what the Church ideally is and must therefore struggle to become. He is arguing against the doomsayers of his day who say that Christianity has run its course. His message is that the Church has but passed through its infancy and that the future is bright with promise, if only people have eyes to see it.

All of the narratives in Acts bear the stamp of the same dominating theme: the third and climactic stage of creation's history has begun. The Christian Church has only to wake up to this fact to survive and prosper. In its own way the community of believers is to relive the saving experiences that took place in Jesus' lifetime.

Thus as Jesus' career began with an outpouring of the Holy Spirit at his baptism, so the Church got under way by being imbued with the same Holy Spirit in the Pentecost experience (see Acts 2:1–4). As Jesus brought healing to the sick, so Peter and the apostles were empowered by the Risen Lord to do the same (see Acts 3:1-10; 9:32-35; 14:8-18). As Jesus showed special compassion for the poor, so the infant Church willingly embraced poverty (see Acts 2:44–45; 4:32). And as Jesus reached beyond the Jews to bring salvation to the Gentiles, so the Church, with Peter (see Acts 10), must learn to do the same.

Luke's sweeping vision of the Church's role in history, as well as his unbounded optimism for the future, caught on. The Church did not cave in before the problems that beset it when Luke wrote. Instead the Church was born anew, along the very lines sketched in Luke's writings. Today we continue to go to Luke, not primarily for historical data about the origins of Christianity but for what Luke wants to share: his breathtaking vision of what the Church is meant to be.

# John

## "In the Beginning Was the Word"

John's Gospel was written about ten years after the Gospels of Matthew and Luke, around 95 A.D. John stands alone on several counts; he does not repeat the familiar terrain of the synoptic Gospels. For example, in John's Gospel there is no infancy story in the style of Matthew and Luke. John the Baptist gives testimony about Jesus, but there is no mention of the baptism of Jesus. The Fourth Gospel also does not contain an account of the Transfiguration or the institution of the Eucharist.

Most of John's miracle stories and summaries of Jesus' words are new, compared to the other Gospels. The magnificent poetry and prose of the prologue (see 1:1–18) is unique to John. So are these stories: the wedding feast at Cana (see 2:1–12); the conversation with Nicodemus (see 2:23—3:21); the Samaritan woman at the well (see 4:1–42); the man born blind (see 9:1–41); the raising of Lazarus (see 11:1–44); and Jesus' washing of his disciples' feet (see 13:1–20).

### The Divinity of Jesus

Above all, John is the Evangelist of Jesus' divinity. Although Mark affirms Jesus to be the "Son of God" and Luke and Matthew uphold the divinity of Jesus even more emphatically, John is strongest of all. He begins by identifying Jesus as existing with God before creation, climaxing his narrative by having Jesus openly claim divinity: "Very truly, I tell you, before Abraham was, I am" (8:58); "The Father and I are one" (10:30). (The many "I am" phrases in the Gospel echo and re-echo the name of Israel's God, Yahweh, "I am" or "I am who am.") In contrast to Mark's account of the passion, John shows Jesus regally calm and purposeful as he confronts death, fully in command of the situation right up to the end.

This unusual Gospel, so unlike the other three, comes from a group of Jewish Christians in Asia Minor or Syria. Their focus is on the divinity of Jesus. Although the author of the Gospel does not deny Jesus' humanity, some of its readers, as we will see in another chapter, downplay that humanity so much that it seems not to exist. In this regard the Johannine community (also called the Community of the Beloved Disciple) is distinctly different from the other first-century churches. The members of this community, however, acknowledge the sincerity of other Christians and pray that the others will join them and accept their more exalted understanding of Jesus. This prayer is reflected in a familiar passage: "I have other sheep that do not belong to this fold. I must bring them also, and they will listen to my voice. So there will be one flock, one shepherd" (John 10:16–17).

So who was this "Beloved Disciple"? He seems to have been a disciple associated with the later ministry of Jesus in Jerusalem. Appearing for the first time at the Last Supper (see 13:23), the disciple was apparently unremarkable during Jesus' ministry but gradually rose to importance in the Johannine community. Eventually he became an important leader and witness testifying to Jesus (see 21:24).

## Jesus the Jew

John's Gospel begins with a prologue (see 1:1–18). The Word (Jesus) was God from all eternity. And the Word became flesh and "from his fullness we have all received" (1:16). Yet many rejected Jesus (see 1:11). The "Book of Signs," as it is called (1:19 through 12:50), presents Jesus' revealing his divinity only to be rejected by many. The signs begin with Jesus' changing water into wine (see 2:1–11) and climax with the raising of Lazarus (see 11:1–44). The ultimate sign is Jesus triumphant, even on the cross.

We do not get far into John's Gospel before we find a marked difference from the other three. In Matthew, Mark and Luke, Jesus cleanses the Temple during the last week of his life. In John, however, Jesus performs the cleansing at the very beginning of his ministry (see 2:13–25). Remembering that the Gospels are faith-proclamations, not standard biographies, we can better appreciate John's intention to present this story right away to set the stage for other stories connected with feasts of the Jews.

The Johannine Christians had been expelled from the synagogues. (The story of the man born blind in chapter 9 reflects the situation of the members of John's community.) Thus the Evangelist wants to reassure his community that they had lost nothing by this excommunication. In chapters 5 through 10 the Evangelist shows Jesus as fulfilling in himself the meanings of various Jewish feasts. In chapter 5 Jesus heals and gives life on the Sabbath, and he does so on his own divine authority. In chapter 6, Jesus multiplies loaves at Passover. Jesus proclaims himself the Bread of Life, replacing the manna that fed the Israelites in the wilderness.

Chapters 7 through 10 present two other feasts: Sukkoth (Tabernacles or Booths, the autumn festival) and Hanukkah. The former includes prayers for rain and the offering of large quantities of water to God. Jesus promises to those who believe in him "living water," the Spirit he would pour out on his Church after his resurrection. At this feast huge torches illuminated the portion of the Temple known as the Court of the Women, and it is in this setting that Jesus proclaims himself the "light of the world." Hanukkah celebrates the rededication of the Temple and its altar at the time of the Maccabees, and it is at this feast that Jesus says that he is the one consecrated by the Father.

As we read John's Gospel we cannot help but notice the antagonism displayed against "the Jews." We must be careful, however, to understand this term correctly. It has too often been used as a warrant for anti-Semitism, and clearly this could not have been the Evangelist's intention. Jesus was a Jew. So were Mary, his mother, and all the apostles. The members of the Evangelist's community were also Jews who had faith in Jesus.

The Church's Good Friday liturgy used to include a prayer for the "perfidious Jews," but Pope John XXIII changed that prayer to a one for those who were "the first to hear the word of God." So it is best to understand the term "the Jews" in John's Gospel as applying to the Jewish leadership who condemned Jesus (and later threw the Jewish Christians out of the synagogues).

## Jesus the Lamb of God

The Last Supper in John is unlike the meal in the synoptic Gospels. Rather than eating a meal Jesus is presented washing the feet of his disciples and discoursing at length. In these chapters John presents themes about the Eucharist without retelling the story of its first celebration. Jesus gives an example of service and tells the disciples to love one another and to stay in union with him, as do branches with a vine. He gives them his farewell gift of peace, and he prays for them.

John again takes liberty with the timing of Jesus' death. The Synoptics tell us that the Last Supper was a Passover meal and that Jesus died on the day of Passover. John, however, moves the events up one day. The Last Supper is not a Passover meal, and Jesus dies on the Preparation Day for Passover. The reason for this variation is not historical but theological. On the Preparation Day lambs by the thousands were ritually slain for the upcoming Passover meals. In John, Jesus dies while the lambs are being slain, emphasizing, as John the Baptist had testified (see 1:36), that Jesus is the Lamb of God, the sacrifice of our redemption.

Even as the sacrificial Lamb, however, Jesus remains the divine Son of God, and John reminds us of this in a short note we might easily overlook. When the soldiers come to arrest Jesus he asks who they want. They reply "Jesus of Nazareth," to which Jesus answered, "I am he." His use of the divine name I AM for himself causes the soldiers to step back and fall to the ground (genuflect). Jesus has to ask them their purpose again before they finally do arrest him (see 18:4–8).

## A Canonical Addition

When we examine the three letters of John we will see that the Community of the Beloved Disciple eventually disintegrated when many of its members drifted away into heresy, insisting on Jesus' divinity without acknowledging his humanity. Some also misunderstood the commandment "Love one another," deciding all kinds of behavior were acceptable so long as they "loved" one another. A remnant of the original community remained true to the Gospel. Ironically, this remnant of the Johannine community, which had once sought to increase the understanding of Christ's divinity so that others might join with them, eventually had to seek union with the larger Church.

Although John 21 was likely added to John's Gospel almost immediately after it was written (John 20:30–31 is an obvious ending), the Church has always accepted this chapter as part of the canonical Gospel of John. A single issue seems to have necessitated this addition to an already finished text. In John 21, Peter is designated head of the Church. Although this was already obvious in the other communities, the Johannine community had always looked instead to the Beloved Disciple as its leader. It seems likely that the Beloved Disciple had just died when these verses were added. Thus did the Johannine community shift its allegiance to the larger Church, represented by Peter.

## Many Things Left Out

Like the other Evangelists, John chooses to report those things he judges best encourage faith in Jesus. But he realizes he could never tell the complete story: "There are also many other things that Jesus did; if every one of them were written down, I suppose that the world itself could not contain the books that would be written" (John 21:25).

# Paul

## A Fascinating Maverick

There can be no doubt that in his day many if not most Christians regarded Paul as a maverick. To some he must have been fascinating, able to stand toe to toe with the apostles and win his point in spite of their evident misgivings. To others he undoubtedly seemed dangerous, stretching the gospel's meaning beyond the breaking point.

Paul did not know Jesus in the same way the Twelve Apostles did. For the Twelve, the resurrection of Jesus confirmed much of what they already knew about him from personal experience. Paul, however, knew Jesus only as the risen Christ, or "the Anointed One." In understanding Jesus as Savior, the apostles tended to work almost entirely from within their background and experience as fervent Jews. They thus proclaimed Jesus primarily as the "Messiah of Israel." But Paul quickly went beyond Judaic thought patterns, affirming Jesus to be the God-sent Savior of all humankind.

### Paul the Jew

Paul was born around 10 A.D. and grew up as a Diaspora Jew in the city of Tarsus in the Roman province of Cilicia, in what is now southwestern Turkey. The language of the streets of Tarsus, even with its large Jewish population, was Greek, and Paul was fluent in it. He also knew some Hebrew and Latin. Thus when Paul journeyed into Greek-speaking cities of the Roman Empire as a missionary he felt right at home. Having grown up in a large city, Paul understood the social structure of urban populations.

Paul (a Roman name) was one name of the future apostle. He also was known by his Jewish name, Saul. Paul was of the tribe of Benjamin, and it is not surprising that he would bear the name of the most famous member of that tribe, King Saul. Paul was a Roman citizen by birth, although we do not know by which of several possible means this was true.

Paul was a Jew and thus was learned in the Torah and diligent in its practice. For a time he thought Jews who became Christians were heretics and he persecuted them. Paul's dramatic conversion took place about 36 A.D., six years after Jesus' death. Just as he had once zealously tried to stamp out the Church, Paul devoted all his zeal after his conversion to proclaiming that Jesus is the Messiah.

## Paul the Missionary

Paul undertook three extensive missionary journeys, across Western Asia and Eastern Europe, and he walked most of this incredible distance! Early on, finding non-Jews attracted to Christianity, Paul took up the matter of Gentile converts with the other apostles in Jerusalem. In keeping with the purpose of Acts, Luke undoubtedly put the best possible light on this meeting (see Acts 15:5–29). But the outcome was clearly in Paul's favor. However reluctant the other apostles might have been, Paul was permitted to make converts of non-Jews without requiring them to accept Judaism as well. This was a major turning point for Christianity.

On his second missionary journey Paul suddenly changed his party's plan to visit Jewish centers of the Diaspora and instead led them directly in pursuit of Gentile converts in Macedonia and Greece. Despite some harrowing experiences he met with great success, establishing Christian communities among the Philippians, the Thessalonians and the Corinthians—communities to which he would later address pastoral letters that became part of the New Testament.

During his third journey Paul wrote his Letter to the Galatians, a Gentile church he had previously founded. In this letter, his most vehement and one of his most incisive, Paul makes a frontal attack on the lingering criticism he continued to receive from Jewish Christians—namely that his notion of "Gentile" Christianity is less than the real thing. Paul doesn't mince words: "You foolish Galatians! Who has bewitched you? It was before your eyes that Jesus Christ was publicly exhibited as crucified! The only thing I want to learn from you is this: Did you receive the Spirit by doing the works of the law or by believing what you heard? Are you so foolish? Having started with the Spirit, are you now ending with the flesh? Did you experience so much for nothing?—if it really was for nothing. Well then, does God supply you with the Spirit and work miracles among you by your doing the works of the law, or by your believing what you heard?" (3:1–5)

Having returned from his third missionary journey in 58 A.D., Paul visited Jerusalem and got into serious trouble. A rumor spread that he had taken a non-Jew into the Temple with him, a desecration that carried the death penalty according to Jewish law. A lynch mob gathered, but Paul was rescued by Roman soldiers. The Romans were about to send him for trial by the Jewish Sanhedrin when warning came of a plot to assassinate him along the way. Paul was then moved under heavy escort to a Roman citadel outside Jerusalem, where he awaited a hearing—in vain—for more than two years. Finally he played his trump card; as a Roman citizen by birth he appealed for a trial in Rome itself.

As we have seen, Luke's account of Paul ends with Paul's arrival in Rome. Although Paul officially was under house arrest, waiting for trial, he apparently had the freedom to come and go. However, we do not know the outcome. Second-century writings say he was acquitted and set free. If so, he possibly made one more missionary journey, to Spain, before his final arrest and execution in Rome in approximately 67 A.D. during the persecution under Nero.

As the "Apostle of the Gentiles," Paul must be credited for releasing Christianity from its early dependence on Judaism. His insistence that salvation comes by faith in Christ and not by adherence to Jewish law and practices eventually took hold, paving the way for Christianity's historic success among people of all nations.

## Paul the Theologian

In comparison to the Gospels, which are written as stories, Paul's letters can be difficult and frustrating to read. But Paul's writings are not intended to give a rounded summary of the Christian message. They are for the most part hastily written instructions regarding pastoral problems of particular first-century churches, but Paul also addresses moral issues as well as questions about God's plan of salvation.

Paul's preaching focuses on the cross, the resurrection and the Second Coming of Christ. Examples of this emphasis are found in Philippians 2:6–11; 2 Corinthians 5:14–15; and Romans 8:34 and 14:9. 1 Corinthians 15:3–4 expresses it like a creed: "For I handed on to you as of first importance what I in turn had received: that Christ died for our sins in accordance with the scriptures, and that he was buried, and that he was raised on the third day in accordance with the scriptures."

For Paul the resurrection of Jesus is essential: "For if the dead are not raised, then Christ has not been raised. If Christ has not been raised, your faith is futile and you are still in your sins. Then those also who have died in Christ have perished. If for this life only we have hoped in Christ, we are of all people most to be pitied. But in fact Christ has been raised from the dead, the first fruits of those who have died" (1 Corinthians 15:16–20).

In his early preaching and writing Paul clearly expects the Second Coming of Jesus soon. In his very first letter, 1 Thessalonians, Paul expresses his longing for the Second Coming and seems to expect to be alive when Jesus returns (see 1 Thessalonians 4:15 and 1 Corinthians 15:51-52). Later in life, however, Paul comes to recognize that he probably will die before Jesus returns.

Were computers available in Paul's day his prison record would be a lengthy printout indeed. Paul, prisoner for the sake of Christ Jesus, was himself unsure at times whether release or execution awaited him (see Philippians 1:20–23). Nonetheless, despite his periods of incarceration Paul was committed to corresponding with the churches he founded.

Thirteen letters in the New Testament are "of Paul." In fact the Apostle to the Gentiles is responsible for nearly half the New Testament. The order of the letters in our Bibles is not chronological; those addressed to congregations precede those to individuals. Within each of these groups the order is roughly by descending length.

Seven letters "of Paul" are directly from Paul, if not from his hand. (Paul used scribes because his own handwriting was poor.) These seven letters are Romans, 1 Corinthians, 2 Corinthians, Galatians, Philippians, 1 Thessalonians and Philemon. Disciples of Paul may have composed the other six, confident they were teaching as Paul himself would have taught.

The technical term for writing in the name of another person is *pseudepigraphy*. The practice is wrong only if it intends to deceive the readers. Paul's disciples, however, did not mean to deceive; they were inspired by God to write letters to convey what they believed Paul would have said were he still alive. Thus most scholars think disciples of Paul wrote 1 Timothy, 2 Timothy and Titus. About 80 percent think this is the case with the Letter to the Ephesians, 60 percent with the Letter to the Colossians, and only a slight majority with 2 Thessalonians.

Such uncertainties regarding authorship need not disturb us. Our faith in the Scriptures is directed to the content of the writings themselves, not to their human authors. Knowing the author of a given work certainly can help us understand its meaning, which is why scholars continue to investigate such matters. Still, certainty about the true author is not required for getting at the true Word of God.

Paul's overall contribution to our understanding of what God accomplished in Jesus is immense. In a very real sense Paul was the Church's first theologian. He probed the deepest meaning of Jesus, not only from the viewpoint of a devout Jew but even more from the viewpoint of a citizen of the world. In Jesus' cross and resurrection Paul found the key to the whole of human existence: "If anyone is in Christ, there is a new creation; everything old has passed away; see, everything has become new...that is, in Christ God was reconciling the world to himself" (2 Corinthians 5:17, 19).

# The Other New Testament Letters

## Providing Theological Standards

Books were added to the Bible one by one as each came to be recognized and accepted by the Church as the Word of God. As time went on, however, it was thought wise to group the books according to a unified plan. Traditionally the New Testament letters were divided into two groups: those of Paul and those not of Paul. Each of the Pauline letters was addressed to a particular church community (Corinth, Thessalonica and Rome) or a particular person (Timothy, Titus and Philemon). The non-Pauline letters were more general; they seemed addressed to all Christians rather than a particular church or person. Thus the non-Pauline letters came to be known simply as the *catholic*, or *universal*, letters. These include three letters of John, two of Peter, one of James and one of Jude. The Letter to the Hebrews is not by Paul, nor is it usually grouped with the catholic letters. We examine it first.

### The Letter to the Hebrews

The author of Hebrews is unknown, but almost certainly it is not Paul. However, as we stressed in the last chapter, our faith in the Scriptures is directed to the content of the writings, not to their human authors. Certainty about the identity of the true author is not required for getting at the true Word of God.

Hebrews almost certainly was composed some years after Paul's death in approximately 67 A.D. Most likely it was written around 85 A.D. As the title indicates, its primary concern is Jewish Christians: the "Hebrews" of the title. These believers were especially discouraged as a result of the destruction of Jerusalem and Christianity's continuing drift from the Jewish religion. Indeed the times had to be especially difficult for Christians whose thinking and background remained strongly wedded to Old Testament institutions such as the Temple, the priesthood and Judaic sacrifices.

The author of the Letter to the Hebrews confronts this difficult situation with deep compassion and insight, thereby smoothing the transition for Christianity as a whole from a Jewish to a Gentile church. In effect the author maintains that the underlying values formerly attached to the Jewish Temple, the Jewish priesthood and Jewish sacrifices are not done away with in the Christian Church. Rather, their meaning and continuing value are elevated to a higher level. As the reigning Messiah, Jesus now endures forever as the one and only High Priest of heaven and earth. His death on the cross is a sacrifice so all-encompassing that further temple sacrifices have become unnecessary. Because Jesus summed up in his life, death and resurrection all that Jewish ritual aspired to accomplish, Judaism has found its highest and most perfect expression in Christianity.

## The Letters of John

Of the three letters of John, the second and third are so brief—hardly a page long—that they seem to have little importance. Their inclusion in the canon of the New Testament, however, testifies to their historical importance for early Christianity. Combined with the longer First Letter of John, these works mark a crucial turning point in Christian doctrine. All three make sense only if we assume that at the time of their composition a major debate was going on in the Church about the truth of the line of thinking we find detailed in the Gospel of John.

The First Letter of John is anonymous; the second and third are written by an author who identifies himself only as "the elder." It is most likely that these three letters are by the author of the Gospel of John. While united with other Christians in essentials, "Johannine" Christians especially prized notions of Jesus uniquely reflected in the Gospel of John. For example, they strongly emphasized that Jesus pre-existed as the eternal Son of God and that the Holy Spirit holds a central place in the governance and daily life of the Church.

The three letters of John concern a division in the early Church, one apparently centered among Johannine Christians themselves. Specifically, there were some who emphasized Jesus' divinity to such an extreme that they regarded Jesus' humanness to be of little importance. These extremists felt so secure in their oneness with the Holy Spirit that they considered themselves to be sinless in the eyes of God. The author of the letters denounces these notions as false, arguing from ideas echoed in John's Gospel.

## The Letter of James

The Letter of James may have been written by James, head of the church in Jerusalem. If so it must be dated before his martyrdom in 62 A.D. On the other hand the letter may have been written later and ascribed to James, because some of the materials actually derive from his teachings.

The Letter of James is quite rambling. In fact, some scholars suggest this is not a letter at all but a collection of fragments that accurately reflect the Jewish Christian tradition of Jerusalem. It resembles much of the Old Testament wisdom literature in that it moves reflectively from topic to topic without a central, unifying theme.

Of particular interest is what James says about the relationship between believing in the gospel and living out one's belief. James insists that faith in Jesus of itself does not bring salvation: "Faith apart from works is barren" (2:20). That there is tension with Paul's theology cannot be denied: "A person is justified not by the works of the law but through faith in Jesus Christ" (Galatians 2:16). On balance we find that Paul also insists that good deeds must necessarily follow if one has true faith. Still, we cannot gloss over the fact that James, a leader of the Jewish-Christian Church, looked at matters differently than did Paul, the leader of Gentile Christians.

## The Letters of Peter and Jude

The letter we call 1 Peter is addressed by the apostle Peter to "the exiles of the Dispersion in Pontus, Galatia, Cappadocia, Asia, and Bithynia" (1:1). It is an encyclical letter sent by the church at Rome (code name: Babylon) to a group of churches in Asia Minor. Catholic scholars generally date the First Letter of Peter about 64

A.D., the same year Peter the Apostle was martyred, but that is by no means certain. Many non-Catholic scholars argue that it was written later and was therefore only attributed to Peter. At any rate the letter encourages Christians to persevere in the face of persecution, pointing out that baptism commits a person to holiness of life and fidelity to the very end.

There is little doubt that the Second Letter of Peter was written by someone other than Peter the Apostle around the end of the first century A.D. or slightly later. It closely parallels the Letter of Jude, which also is dated to the last years of the first century. Both works are concerned with defections and false teachings in the Church, and both strongly uphold the doctrine of the final coming of Christ.

## Viewed as a Whole

New Testament letters other than the works of Paul witness to the diversity of Christian theologies that existed from the very start. Viewed as a whole these books make it clear that there is no single way to express humanly what God has accomplished in Jesus Christ. At the same time these works provide the Church sure standards by which to judge Christian theologies today—theologies that in their own way continue to probe the unfathomable mystery of Christ.

# Revelation

## The Gospel in Times
## of Persecution and Suffering

When Catholics are asked "What is the Book of Revelation about?" most will likely answer "The end of the world." When Catholics are asked, "Have you ever read the Book of Revelation?" most will likely answer "No."

A poll some years ago showed that more Catholics had read at least one commentary on the Book of Revelation by a fundamentalist preacher than had read the book itself. For fundamentalist Christians the Book of Revelation is prophecy (in the sense of prediction) about events in the near future. Some fundamentalists suggest that John, the author of the book (see 1:1, 4), was physically transported from his own first century A.D. to our near future to witness events at the end of the world. Others fancifully but incorrectly interpret Revelation's symbols as describing ballistic missiles, Apache attack helicopters and nuclear blasts.

A standard fundamentalist interpretation of the "final days" has several features. The Temple of Solomon will be rebuilt (presumably by tearing down Islam's sacred site, the Dome of the Rock). Then will come a leader, the Antichrist, who along with Satan will establish a world religion. And a cataclysmic battle will be fought in the valley of Megiddo, into which more than 200 million soldiers will have somehow managed to squeeze.

Sadly, many Catholics have accepted these widely circulated ideas. They think the Book of Revelation is about linear history and "foretells" our future. In reality the message of the Book of Revelation brings hope born of the knowledge of God's love, our surety in time of trouble.

Like our ancestors in faith twenty centuries ago, we Christians of the twenty-first century live in troubled times. Certainly the challenges we face are different, but Revelation's message remains the same: The Lord Jesus is victorious and all who are faithful to him will share in his victory. Revelation does not promise an escape from pain and suffering. Rather it promises that the Lord Jesus is always with us and gives us strength to endure whatever comes.

## A Prophetic Message

What, then, is the Book of Revelation? The complete answer may be phrased: "The Book of Revelation is a letter to be read at the liturgy. It contains a prophetic message written in the style called *apocalypse*." That's quite a mouthful, so let's break it down.

The Book of Revelation is a letter, very much like those of Paul. First there is the ancient style of salutation: "John to the seven churches that are in Asia," followed by the blessing, "grace and peace" (1:4). Then seven individual congregations are addressed specifically ( chapters 2 and 3). The letter concludes in a standard Christian way: "The grace of the Lord Jesus be with all the saints" (22:21). Paul wrote his letters to substitute for his physical presence. He wrote back to Christian communities he had established and ahead to the church at Rome. In the same way John, in exile on the island Patmos, used a letter as a substitute for being present to the churches. Intending his letter to be read aloud to the worshiping congregation, John invokes a blessing on "the one who reads aloud" and on "those who hear and who keep what is written in it" (1:3).

The Book of Revelation is prophecy. Like the Old Testament prophets before him, John spoke the word of the Lord to exhort God's people to follow him faithfully. His message to his fellow first-century Christians was not about our twenty-first century, however, but about the demands of discipleship in their own time and place. The urgency John felt is clear throughout the book. Beginning in 1:3 he tells his readers "the time is near."

## Form and Authorship

The Book of Revelation is written as an apocalypse. Like other books of the New Testament, the Book of Revelation throws light on the central truth of the gospel. It does not stand apart from this truth nor add something substantially different. One commentator uses a musical analogy: Revelation is the same gospel but it is written in a different key. What makes Revelation distinctive is its use of an unusual literary form called "apocalypse," the Greek word for "revelation."

In previous chapters we have discussed the importance of recognizing the literary form of a work, and we must respect that same distinction here in our understanding of the Book of Revelation. We must be sure not to confuse the devices used in the literary form apocalypse with the message.

Apocalyptic writing flourished in Judaism during the two centuries before Christ and the two centuries after his death. Toward the start of this period, for example, we meet apocalypse in the Book of Daniel. The Book of Revelation is the sole New Testament example of this ancient literary form, which uses many symbols to convey its message. The symbols are normally borrowed from familiar Old Testament works. In the case of Revelation the symbols are borrowed most frequently from Ezekiel, Zechariah and Daniel. For those who knew the Old Testament Scriptures, the symbolism of the Book of Revelation was readily understood.

The author of Revelation was an otherwise unknown Jewish Christian prophet named John. He was neither John the son of Zebedee (he writes of the apostles without mentioning himself as one of their number; see 21:14), nor the author of the Gospel and the Letters of John (whose Greek is excellent, while Revelation's Greek is very poor). John was indeed a very common name among the early Christians. Ironically, the assumption that the author of Revelation was the apostle John may have facilitated the book's acceptance by the Church into the canon of Scripture.

The date of composition is probably around 95 A.D., during the last years of the emperor Domitian. Roman persecution of Christians waned after Nero's death in 68 A.D. but broke out anew in the province of Asia in the later years of the reign of the emperor Domitian (81-96 A.D.). In fact some scholars think the emperor himself may have initiated the persecution. (He did style himself *dominus et deus*, "Lord and God," titles Christians would not use except for Christ.) More likely, the churches of the seven large cities of the province of Asia were suffering at the hands of local officials who wanted to curry favor with the emperor and would have looked most unfavorably on the Christians' refusal to join in emperor worship.

Like the author of Daniel before him, John wished to encourage believers to hold steadfast in faith even in the face of possible martyrdom. His message, quite simply, is that God's power is greater than Rome's and that in the end Christianity will triumph. Christ assures untold rewards at his final coming for those who persevere in faith.

## Concerning the Future

In the first three chapters of Revelation, after establishing that he speaks in the name of Christ himself, the author addresses seven church communities in turn, alternately chiding and encouraging them. Of special interest is the timelessness of these admonitions. The same strengths and weaknesses identified by the author of the Book of Revelation have been experienced in Christian communities throughout the centuries and can be found mirrored around us today. The fidelity of the churches of Smyrna and Philadelphia, for example, is present again in the lives of faithful Christians today. And, as he did the churches of Sardis and Laodicea, the Lord challenges us to acknowledge the ways we fail to repent and live the gospel fully.

The vision of "what must take place" actually begins with the fourth chapter. The author first grounds his message in heaven, before the throne of God. Then by the use of images, symbols and numbers he proceeds to make known the substance of his revelation concerning the future. Bearing in mind that the language is figurative, not literal, it is useless to try to "picture" the scene exactly as the author describes it. The symbols in Revelation are not drawn from our modern world but from the language and experiences of the ancient world; there simply is no modern equivalent for the literary form apocalypse. Odd combinations of ordinary things (such as the locusts with scorpion's tails and human heads in 9:7–11) do not reflect reality; they are only a means of communication.

Revelation, written in a time of persecution, views the Roman Empire as a beastly harlot drunk with the blood of martyrs. (Quite a different view from the attitude of respect and offering of prayers for the secular rulers in other New Testament writings, such as Romans 13, 1 Peter 2 and 1 Timothy 2.) Still, John does not tell Christians to take up arms. They are to endure persecution and remain faithful to the Lord Jesus, who alone is victorious.

While the modest scope of our book does not allow us to examine the multitude of symbols in Revelation, we can note the following: In all the Scriptures God's message for his people is expressed in the words of true human authors—and this is no less true for the Book of Revelation. The meanings John attached to the symbols he used are essential for understanding Revelation's message. God's chosen people, represented by the woman of chapter 12, have given birth to the Messiah and, through him, the Church. The dragon bent on destroying the woman's offspring is Satan, who is indeed powerful but has already been defeated by Christ and can therefore be defeated by Christ's followers. The Roman Empire is symbolized by the two beasts of chapter 13 and Babylon in chapter 17. In chapters 18 and 19 God's future vengeance upon this evil state is assured. Likewise assured is the blessedness of martyrs at the final coming of Christ.

One symbol in Revelation deserves special attention: the number 666 (see 13:18), which is the name of a man. Ancient languages used letters to express numbers. For example, consider our set of Roman numerals. The numerical equivalents of the name and title "Nero Caesar" add up to 666. It is clear that the meaning of this symbol is the name of the first emperor to persecute Christians. In turn the number is applied to Domitian because in persecuting the Church he has become "another Nero."

We must resist the temptation to "find" in 666 the name of history's other beasts. We also must avoid the fundamentalist fantasy that the beast in Revelation is alive today. John understood the meaning of 666 to be Nero, the archetype of all persecutors of the Church. Thus only analogously can we apply 666 to other persecutors of God's people. The Christians in Nazi Germany or the Soviet Union, for example, could turn to the Book of Revelation and find encouragement. Like the Christians of the province of Asia centuries before, faithful followers of Christ in Nazi Germany and the

U.S.S.R. suffered many things, including martyrdom, at the hands of "other Neros"—Adolf Hitler and Josef Stalin.

The concluding chapters of the Book of Revelation portray the happiness of heaven at the end of time: "Death will be no more; mourning and crying and pain will be no more.... See, I am making all things new" (21:4–5).

# Conclusion

The Bible is the book of the Church, the people of God. In this brief overview we have outlined the contents of the two components of the Bible: the Old Testament and the New Testament. We have seen that the Christian Bible owes its origins to the early Christian Church. These Sacred Scriptures reflect the faith understanding of this community during its birth and infancy. Thus in no sense may the Scriptures be viewed as having a life of their own separate from the community whose faith they express. The Scriptures must be prayed and responded to as an integral part of the Church's ongoing life and journey through history.

Prior to the Second Vatican Council very little Scripture was read during Mass. On Sundays and the great feast days, readings from the Old Testament were virtually nonexistent, and the same small selection of readings from the Gospels and the New Testament letters was repeated year after year. What's more, the readings were in Latin. Members of the congregation were left to follow along as best they could with the help of a missal in English.

This changed, however, with important liturgical reforms brought about by the Second Vatican Council (1962–1965). As noted in the *Constitution on the Sacred Liturgy* (one of the primary documents of Vatican II), "In the restoration and promotion of the sacred liturgy the full and active participation by all the people is the aim to be considered before all else" (#14). Thus the Council decreed that the selection of biblical readings in the Mass be greatly expanded. All four Gospels, for example, are now read extensively over a three-year period. In addition an abundance of selections from books of both Testaments is presented on a cyclic basis. In the Mass we collectively pray and respond to God's Word as nourishment for our lives as individual Christians and as the community of believers—the Church.

We also need to reflect upon God's Word in our daily lives, not just at Mass on Sunday. Spending just a few minutes each day getting to know the Bible will remind us of God's ever-present covenant love. For as Hebrews reminds us, "Indeed, the word of God is living and active" (4:12).

# Biblical Timeline

# Biblical Timeline

*The timeline below is merely a guide to connecting some of the events in the Bible (below the line) with other events taking place in the ancient world (above the line). It is not meant to be comprehensive or definitive, and many dates are approximate.*

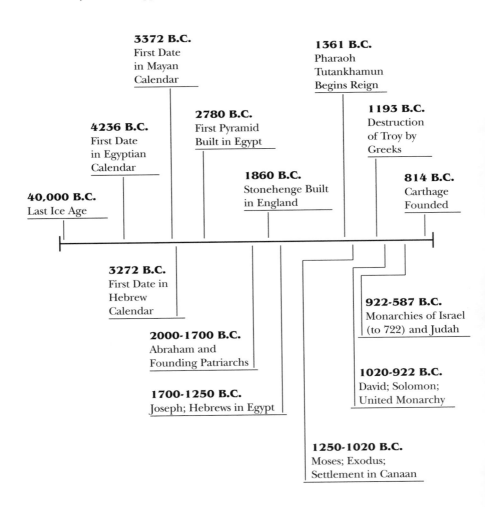

**3372 B.C.**
First Date
in Mayan
Calendar

**1361 B.C.**
Pharaoh
Tutankhamun
Begins Reign

**2780 B.C.**
First Pyramid
Built in Egypt

**1193 B.C.**
Destruction
of Troy by
Greeks

**4236 B.C.**
First Date
in Egyptian
Calendar

**1860 B.C.**
Stonehenge Built
in England

**814 B.C.**
Carthage
Founded

**40,000 B.C.**
Last Ice Age

**3272 B.C.**
First Date in
Hebrew
Calendar

**2000-1700 B.C.**
Abraham and
Founding Patriarchs

**922-587 B.C.**
Monarchies of Israel
(to 722) and Judah

**1700-1250 B.C.**
Joseph; Hebrews in Egypt

**1020-922 B.C.**
David; Solomon;
United Monarchy

**1250-1020 B.C.**
Moses; Exodus;
Settlement in Canaan

# Biblical Timeline

*The timeline below is merely a guide to connecting some of the events in the Bible (below the line) with other events taking place in the ancient world (above the line). It is not meant to be comprehensive or definitive, and many dates are approximate.*

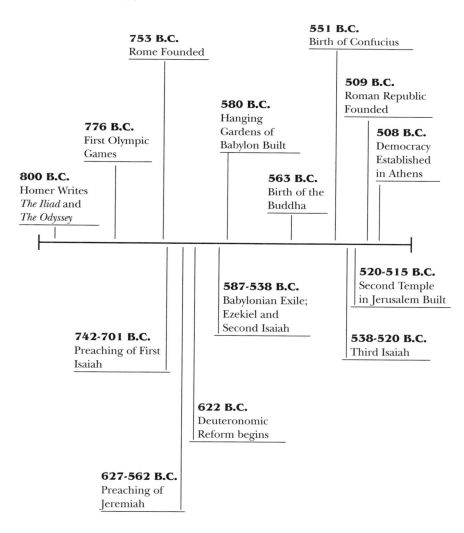

**800 B.C.**
Homer Writes
*The Iliad* and
*The Odyssey*

**776 B.C.**
First Olympic
Games

**753 B.C.**
Rome Founded

**580 B.C.**
Hanging
Gardens of
Babylon Built

**563 B.C.**
Birth of the
Buddha

**551 B.C.**
Birth of Confucius

**509 B.C.**
Roman Republic
Founded

**508 B.C.**
Democracy
Established
in Athens

**742-701 B.C.**
Preaching of First
Isaiah

**587-538 B.C.**
Babylonian Exile;
Ezekiel and
Second Isaiah

**520-515 B.C.**
Second Temple
in Jerusalem Built

**538-520 B.C.**
Third Isaiah

**622 B.C.**
Deuteronomic
Reform begins

**627-562 B.C.**
Preaching of
Jeremiah

# Biblical Timeline

*The timeline below is merely a guide to connecting some of the events in the Bible (below the line) with other events taking place in the ancient world (above the line). It is not meant to be comprehensive or definitive, and many dates are approximate.*

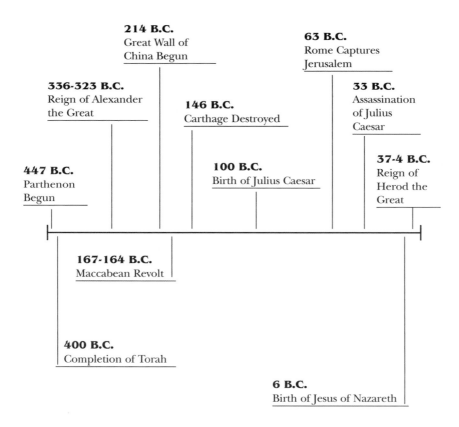

**214 B.C.**
Great Wall of
China Begun

**63 B.C.**
Rome Captures
Jerusalem

**336-323 B.C.**
Reign of Alexander
the Great

**33 B.C.**
Assassination
of Julius
Caesar

**146 B.C.**
Carthage Destroyed

**447 B.C.**
Parthenon
Begun

**100 B.C.**
Birth of Julius Caesar

**37-4 B.C.**
Reign of
Herod the
Great

**167-164 B.C.**
Maccabean Revolt

**400 B.C.**
Completion of Torah

**6 B.C.**
Birth of Jesus of Nazareth

# Biblical Timeline

*The timeline below is merely a guide to connecting some of the events in the Bible (below the line) with other events taking place in the ancient world (above the line). It is not meant to be comprehensive or definitive, and many dates are approximate.*

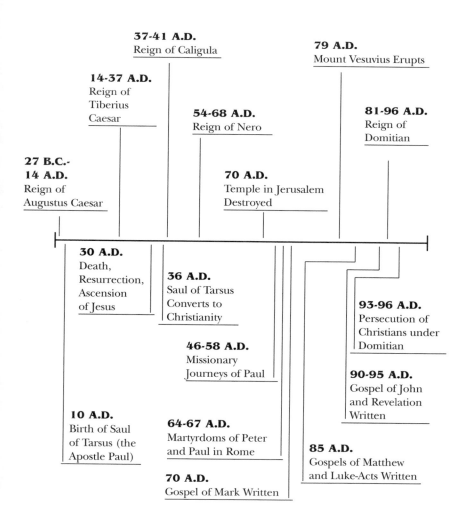

**37-41 A.D.**
Reign of Caligula

**79 A.D.**
Mount Vesuvius Erupts

**14-37 A.D.**
Reign of
Tiberius
Caesar

**54-68 A.D.**
Reign of Nero

**81-96 A.D.**
Reign of
Domitian

**27 B.C.-
14 A.D.**
Reign of
Augustus Caesar

**70 A.D.**
Temple in Jerusalem
Destroyed

**30 A.D.**
Death,
Resurrection,
Ascension
of Jesus

**36 A.D.**
Saul of Tarsus
Converts to
Christianity

**93-96 A.D.**
Persecution of
Christians under
Domitian

**46-58 A.D.**
Missionary
Journeys of Paul

**90-95 A.D.**
Gospel of John
and Revelation
Written

**10 A.D.**
Birth of Saul
of Tarsus (the
Apostle Paul)

**64-67 A.D.**
Martyrdoms of Peter
and Paul in Rome

**85 A.D.**
Gospels of Matthew
and Luke-Acts Written

**70 A.D.**
Gospel of Mark Written

# Also from ACTA Publications

*Invitation to Catholicism*
*Beliefs + Teachings + Practices*
Alice Camille

Everyone from lifelong Catholics to interested non-Catholics will welcome the easy-to-understand, logical explanations found in this overview of Catholic beliefs, teachings and practices. (240-page softcover, $9.95)

*Jesus and His Message*
*An Introduction to the Good News*
Rev. Leo Mahon

A clear, concise introduction to who Jesus was and what he taught, focusing on his ministry of teaching and healing, his passion, death and resurrection. (112-page softcover, $6.95)

*Life in Christ*
*A Catholic Catechism for Adults*
Revs. Gerard Weber and James Killgallon

This bestselling catechism for adults presents all aspects of Catholics teaching in a question and answer manner that is easy to use yet thorough and comprehensive. (327-page softcover, $6.95)

*The Rosary*
*Mysteries of Joy, Light, Sorrow and Glory*
Alice Camille

New reflections on each of the mysteries of the Rosary, including the new Mysteries of Light. This book also offers a concise history of the Rosary and some reflections on its meaning for the new millennium. (112-page softcover, $6.95)

**Available from booksellers or call 800-397-2282**
**(www.actapublications.com)**